I Wonder
An Immigrant's Song

Poems and Essays by Mark Sashine
Poetic Translations by Hal O'Leary

I Wonder
An Immigrant's Song

Poems and Essays by Mark Sashine
Poetic Translations by Hal O'Leary

First Edition

ISBN: 978-1-937449-35-3

Published by:

YAV PUBLICATIONS
ASHEVILLE, NORTH CAROLINA

YAV books may be purchased in bulk for educational, business, fund-raising, or sales promotional use. For information, contact Books@yav.com or phone toll-free 888-693-9365.
Visit our website: www.InterestingWriting.com

3 5 7 9 10 8 6 4 2

Assembled in the United States of America
Published April 2018

For Maria, Nata, and Anna

PREFACE: Aiming High

Mark Sashine

We call this book a biography of the feeling. It is up to the reader to define this feeling after getting to the end of the book. It is the result of cooperation between the two people representing three countries: US, Russia and Ireland. When I was a child Ireland was my favorite country maybe due to poetry or due to the rich and tragic history so similar to the one of my country, Russia. Russian ancient chronicles state that the first ruling dynasty in Russia comes from the Viking king Rurik, which meant O'Rourke as far as I see it; Red Fox in the Russian folklore is called 'the daughter of Patrick', pointing at the right direction. It was not a coincidence that a person from Russia and an Irish-American became soulmates and cooperated in the project. We both aimed high.

Aiming high means sharing the unique vision. This book is a fresh view at the concept of diversity. US have been struggling with this concept for quite a while. It can be also called an identity crisis. There seem to be a push for the formal lining up of the people; let them know English and accept the values. There is also a counter-push; to preserve the 'culture' at any cost. Both approaches seem to lead nowhere. The approach presented in this book is based on human equality.

'All men are created equal'-states the Declaration of Independence. Equality means that every person's contributive voice is to be heard and acknowledged. The voice of the first generation immigrant is of utmost importance because he/she sees things from both perspectives and develops a unique feeling of love and loss at the same time. That feeling can only be communicated on equal footage. The best way to achieve that is to invoke the language of poetry. This immigrant speaks to his new country as an equal. This book is in two languages-English and Russian. Each chapter but 'The Reciprocity' contains the same structure: my poem in Russian, its poetic translation by Hal O'Leary and my supportive essay in English on the topic. 'The Reciprocity' contains a poem by Edgar A. Poe and my translation of it into Russian.

The book is called 'I Wonder'. That is a quintessential fate of an immigrant–the feeling of wonder becomes a sixth sense.

The book is a personal research in an issue of immigration and not a historical reference. It can be used as a supplement in teaching Russian language. All quotes from Russian authors are taken from the publications in the USSR during its existence.

I hereby acknowledge that the poem 'With My Son At The Wall of Communards at Pere La Chaise Cemetery' (chapter 5) was published (with retaining the author's rights for republishing in the book) in the French Magazine Mgv2_86 Proletarian Literature, Oct. 2016. The essay "The Immortals' (chapter 13) was published under the same conditions in its original form under the title "The Apprenticeship' on the website www.OpEdNews.com in Y2012. All illustrations are licensed to use by the standard license from www.ShuterStock.com (with id#given).

Note for the readers-grammarians: The English language of the book is not perfect. But neither is the language of the politicos in Washington. Please, cut us some slack. Feeling cannot be expressed without some faults on the way.

What here shall miss, our toil shall strive to mend

W. Shakespeare, ***Romeo and Juliet,*** Prologue

Contents

Chapter 1

Introduction and Connection

A Rogue Goose

A writer is a rogue goose. All other geese fly in a flock formation; every goose knows his place and the time for honking. The rogue goose is undisciplined. He leaves the formation to have a look at it from aside, roams back and forth, takes a peep at the leader, honks a little bit from behind, and distracts everyone. From this perspective, the writer writes on what he sees; as with the goose, the time passes and he would like to return back to his place, but he discovers that some other bird had taken his place. Thus, he either has to wait until the flock lands to rest or join another flock in emigration. Those-other birds could be cranes, storks or even crows, and if he makes it, he will become a rogue again. Wherever he goes and whatever he does, neither the goose, nor the writer ever reaches a destination or enjoys a landing. There's only Kipling's God of Fair Beginnings and skies above and beyond. And the only way for a writer to make peace with the Deity is through the language of Poetry.

Connection: The Dumbest Age

When I was fifteen and lived in Russia, there was a popular movie *Dubravka*. That was a nickname for thirteen years-old girl. It means 'a patch of young forest'. There was such girl in the US literature too. Her name was Jean Louise Finch, a.k.a. Scout. Both girls went through the same process of coming of age and becoming adults while facing tough problems. Jean Louise faced the matters of love, life, justice and death. Dubravka faced the matters of love, choice, trust and betrayal. The movie was based on a story by Radii Pogodin, the children's writer. Radii means *Radium* in Russian. Russians were very much into physics and nuclear energy in his times. Children were named Radium, Uranium, Icarus, Helium and even Hydrogen, like in this country Native Americans name people Running Deer or Trout Fishing. In the story Dubravka was in the company of older children, who were trying to stage Hans Christian Andersen's "The Snow Queen" in their drama circle. It is a beautiful fairy-tale about love, friendship and sacrifice. Of course, the girls competed for the role of the Queen and there was a big commotion. The boys were all into 'macho behavior'. They argued and irritated each other which did nothing good for the play. Dubravka didn't get a part. She usually sat apart, watching. One day the director of the play, a plain, elderly gentleman with hands so white from age that they seemed transparent, approached her.

"Those high school seniors, they are at the dumbest age," he said. "They don't know that the most beautiful fairy-tale in the world is Cinderella, and the wisest fairy tale is The Emperor's New Clothes. It was Art, that little boy, who pointed out that the Emperor was naked."

That elusive little boy has been following me ever since. There should be a reason why the director decided to speak of art to Dubravka. It took me a long time to figure out that he recognized a diamond where other people could see only a piece of rock.

Chapter 2

Welcome to the Family

Practice Resurrection...

Wendell Berry
The Mad Farmer's Manifesto

СЕМЬЯ

Я роднюсь с эмигрантами первой волны,
С офицерами армии белой.
С молодежью Галлиполи мы сроднены
И забрызганы общею пеной.

Век заходит, нам некуда больше спешить,
Время камни собрать и сложить.
Пароход под охраной на рейде дымит,
Хочет в ссылку скорее отбыть.

Это братья мои не ужились в стране,
Уходя в бесконечный туман.
Эмиграция духа застыла на дне,
Под ночного кошмара дурман.

Я хочу породниться и с теми, кто был
Распинаем за ум и талант.
Жертвы варварства средь безымянных могил
Миллионами рядом лежат.

Я прошусь как в семью к тем, кто в слуги не лез,
Не ходил у убийц в холуях,
Кто у жизни не требовал многих чудес,
Сколь возможно себя сохранял.
Мне родные и те, кто ушел навсегда
Под поганый, глухой шепоток.
Эмиграция третьей волны как вода,
Просочилась—и высох песок.

Я ушел как с семьею с последней волной,
Когда воздух сгустился как дым.
Мы осели на почве планеты чужой,
Только Солнце осталось своим.

Собираю я здесь, у себя за столом,
В новогоднюю лунную ночь,
Умных всех, честных всех, кто не слыл дураком,
Мы прогоним всех демонов прочь.

Наше братство навек, нить единой судьбы
Протянулась сквозь времени бег
Но грохочет в нас эхо великой борьбы:
Силы зла победил человек.

FAMILY

We and the first wave now are family
With Russian emigrants who leave our home
In bond with those of old Gallipoli
Awash and covered by the same sea foam

Our lifetime ends, but nowhere need we speed
It's time to place our options in a row.
It's time that we adopt a different creed.
The ship awaits. We know it's time to go.

My brothers can no longer fit, like me,
The only land and life they ever knew.
The spirit too can slip beneath the sea,
And like a freezing mist, can fade from view.

I'd join the crucified beneath the waves,
The talented and mindful souls they hate,
The millions now who lie in unmarked graves,
The victims of a most barbaric fate.

I'd join, as well, the family of those
Whose stoic lives had kept them free of blame,
Who wanted naught but live the life they chose
Perhaps with little pride but with no shame.

Like those before who left with little cheer,
Like those before who left the mother-land,
The third wave washed ashore to disappear,
Absorbed like water by the burning sand.

And with the faithful, final wave I left
To sense and breathe once more at freedom's flame,
Although with others, still I felt bereft,
Another planet! But the sun-the same.

So now, my friends, on this, a New Year's Eve,
I toast my families who were not fools.
Please feast with me, but here we take our leave,
Pray, let us vow to drive away the ghouls.

And in our everlasting brotherhood,
A single thread of destiny will run
With echoes of the struggles understood
And memories of battles we have won,
We challenge now the evil with the good.

I am an alien. There are illegal aliens, legal aliens, resident aliens, migrant workers, H-1 visa recipients, parolees and many others. We are humans. We all didn't know that we were aliens until we came to the US. In the movie *Alien Nation* aliens, the newcomers were physically different from humans. We are not. Our difference is spiritual; our ways are different, our perceptions are different, our souls are different. That comes from the life experience. I came here from Russia. People left Russia in the 20th Century in waves; each wave was unique. The first wave was during the Civil War 1917–1922 and shortly after that. The casualties of that period were never disclosed but some historians assess those to be of about 14 million people, mainly civilians. That was a huge emigration wave, the first one—about 2–3 million, primarily to Western Europe.

The second wave was after the WWII when many Russians who were moved to Germany by force as *Osterbaiten* (slaves from the East), decided not to return after the Allies liberated them. I am not talking traitors, Nazi collaborators and war criminals. I am talking about ordinary people trapped between loyalties. Many of them chose not to go back and nobody should judge them.

The third wave took place in the 60s and 70s. It was a trickle, a leakage due to the primarily Jewish emigration to Israel after the 6-day's war in 1967. Jews were allowed intermittently to leave the country but they were not allowed to take their property or money with them. They were deprived of their citizenship and harassed. Officially they didn't exist; as if suddenly certain people you knew would disappear into oblivion.

The last wave, the one that brought me to America was in the 1980s, when Soviet system was collapsing and the very physical safety of many people became threatened. Long before Chechnya we had the Sumgait Armenian massacres, pogroms in Almatu, Karabakh, and other bloody skirmishes. We left to safeguard our children.

When people leave their country of birth it is not because they want better economic opportunities or to realize their potential, etc. It is because they are running away from something horrible, unbearable, and murderous. And in running, they become close, a family united in the misfortune. They are my extended family forever. Together we are the Alien Nation.

Then you have a bad weather for a while; not the Hemingway's bad weather but the one inside you. It takes time to collect yourself, to start functioning and make conclusions. You look around and come up with something, anything:

THE REVELATIONS OF THE FIRST GENERATION IMMIGRANT

Времена не выбирают
В них живут и умирают..
А. Кушнер

You don't chose your time
You just live and die in it.

Alexander Kushner

Where is your precipice for the free men?

G. Figuereidu 'Aesop'

Was it Worth It?

In a small New England town I spotted an Italian bakery, entered and ordered coffee. The proprietor, an elderly gentleman with distinctively noble Italian features, watched me for a while and than said,

> "You don't look so good, Mr. First Generation."
> "Well, here one year counts for two. You must know that," I said.
> "Sure, man. But the children are happy, right?"
> "Yes, that's why it's worth it."
> "Let's drink to that."

He pulled out a bottle of Grappa and filled two shots. We drank to the two members of the Nation of the First Generation. The nation in business of going out of business.

Helpless Love

Emigration is always a family affair but one person makes the decision. Sometimes that person doesn't even know that he or she made this decision. Our son made a decision for us when he was 4 years' old.

Russian poet Alexander Pushkin once said, "When you live in the toilet you put up with the stench." In the country of your birth you can put up with a lot of things. You can put up with permanent lines, with communal apartments with one toilet for 10 families, with dull lies in the press, with lousy food, with restricted access for you and your kind to certain professions. You can put up with lawlessness, with the power in the hands of the mobsters, with the moronic evil (courtesy of Stephen King) eating up your life day-by-day. You can even put up with the most horrible thing—the fact that you are not in charge of your own life, that everything, from your birth to your death is predefined. That's because you love the place and all those people. You love the city you were born in, smell of lilac in May and the scatter of the chestnut leaves in the fall. You love the magnificent architecture, music, paintings and literature, the best in the world. It all belongs to you no matter what. That's until your child makes a decision.

Public unrests and the consequences of the nuclear power plant accident threaten your child. Suddenly you realize that this moronic evil you put up with wants your son dead. If you don't do something right now, your son will soon be dead or severely crippled and no one around will give a damn. That is because you are doomed in their minds, the way your ancestors were doomed, those whose bones lie in the pit at the city outskirts where they were shot to death during WWII. You have a new duty now and if there is a chance for your child, that chance is his and you have to provide it.

The decision is unanimous but the process is slow and painful. Through all the humiliations of standing in lines to the authorities, through abuse and harassment, through stupid regulations, through fear of rejection, through giving your humble possessions to friends and relatives (we were allowed only to take out $300 and very limited belongings), through waiting for the permission to leave, you still hope that it is a dream, that you will wake up with all your friends on the beach, laughing and singing.

That's until you start noticing signs. I noticed my sign #1 when the blondish creature lazily remarked while taking our applications to leave,

"Why are you, people leaving? We are not killing you yet."

Then came the sign #2.

"You, folks, shouldn't go to the city street arts festivities. That's for your own safety," said my friend who worked with the police.

"Why?"

"Well, you know how it is now. People of your origin are to be careful nowadays. Everyone is very angry. You know what happened in other cities, right?"

Yes, we knew. In some cities in the East the people of Armenian descent were raped and brutally murdered. In other places that happened to the people of Turkish descent. We are not Turks or Armenians; we are Jews. They are not killing us yet. But people can be angry with us. Other people, our neighbors. They can be angry with us and openly discuss in the newspapers what to do with us. They can write letters to the editors saying that we all are vermin and those letters can be published openly as opinions. We cannot be angry with them. That's how it goes.

Sign #3 comes with the denouncement of your citizenship. You pay the fines, surrender your passport and you are legally dead. You cease to exist. Away you go by train and airplane, no longer a documented person.

At the airport we got our last boot. Hundreds of ethnic Germans sat on the floor in one of the big halls, families and all. They were waiting for visas to the Federal Republic. After 500 years, those farmers were leaving because the mob attacked them and the government didn't help them. I forgot my own misery when I saw them. What a terrible tragedy. For a farmer emigration is not just leaving; it is surrendering his very sense of life. I told them that if I was in charge I would have placed a tank in front of each of those farms, so that they could only stay, plant crops, breed cows, make milk and butter. The words of Friedrich Durrenmatt came to mind:

When your country becomes a coven of criminals and a breeding ground for executioners, wipe its dust from your feet because your love for it is helpless.

Our year's ordeal ended in the two hours' air flight. A van driver brought us to an apartment building in Vienna and drove away. I pushed the button and there was silence.

That's how a technical PhD of thirty three, who could recite Shakespeare and Pushkin by heart, his wife of twenty nine, a mechanical engineer, their four years' old son and mother-in law, sixty eight years old, the WWII veteran and a distinguished surgeon became refugees without a country on a dusky street of Vienna, Austria.

America 'from Sea to Shining Sea'

America is the land of opportunity but only one opportunity that is; an opportunity to be who you really are. Like the mask in the movie 'Mask' it enhances and promotes the already existing features of a character, which really define the personality but had been dormant or not fully realized due the circumstances in the society that person lived in before the emigration. An honest, hardworking individual will become even more honest and hardworking, a petty thief can become a big crook and even a millionaire, a compulsive liar can become a politician, a cheap person can become Scrooge, a deeply religious person can become a preacher, a covert womanizer can become an open philanderer, an unsuccessful rapist can become a real one, a woman, who has only one child can have many and a woman, who does not want children can dedicate herself to herself without guilt or remorse. That is because there is no such thing as American nation, no such thing as a carved-in-stone societal perception on what is good and what is bad, no real sense of belonging to the 'people' as an entity.

When I speak, generations of Russians speak through me whether I want it or not. My language is the language of Nestor, Ivan the Terrible, Peter the Great, Pushkin, Lenin and Stalin. The consciousness I possess is the social consciousness of the farmers of my region even though I am Jewish and never had a farm.

There is no social consciousness in the US, neither is there a generally accepted sense of morality. Instead, there are clusters, groups, territorial customs and individual interests.US resembles the medieval Europe, somewhere in the 15th-16th Centuries.

We went through the INS interview process in Europe and were lucky to be admitted. My first impression of the US was a balloon. A tall, lanky woman was meeting us in the mid-America airport and an enormous balloon floated over her head. The balloon had our names on it. It struck me at the time that I would never use a balloon that way. But it worked; we noticed her.

I got my first job with the small engineering company. The owner was a mechanical buff and somewhat of an environmentalist. That was another piece of luck for us.

There was no problem with my accent because it was only one of many; the company was full of immigrants. Along with the South African, Irish, German and Chinese accents, the Dalmatian☺accent of mine was not that unusual. I still keep it. Thanks to that job my wife could enroll in the university English courses and we settled as real Americans in a small town of about 5000 residents. Our son went out to the street and returned no longer a Russian. Of us four, our son is the first person who speaks English and Spanish much better than Russian and we speak English with him. We both, of course are fluent in English.

Due to the job I got we skipped the usual process of assimilation within the community of the people of the same kind, like in New York, Boston or any other place, where there are big Russian-Jewish settlements. We liked the idea and decided for ourselves that whenever possible we'd be on our own, belong to no group and cherish our independence. We keep this resolution so far, but it is not without a price. Both of us have been relatively successful. I lost my first job, got several others. We moved several times. My wife studied and worked full time. Our son is an adult, married, and has a good job. Time to reflect:

The everyday life

I have six honest serving men,
They taught me all I knew.
Their names are What and Why and When,
And How and Where and Who

R. Kipling

Food

Americans eat everything. That is they are offered food in abundance, but the quality of food is not as important as its price. Thus it is very low. Milk is not milk, cheese is not cheese, juice is not juice. Everything tastes the like hay. Sauces mask the blandness. But the price is low and people eat that stuff. I still cannot eat frozen food, and 80% of the things in the supermarkets, drink Coke and Pepsi. Try drinking Pepsi warm. Good food is either very rare or very expensive. That's why it is not true that people get fat because they don't eat right. They don't eat right no matter what; it's not their choice, period. It's the same with the drinks. Cheap beer is in abundance and nobody cares how bad it is for you. I agree with Ralph Nader that fast food is a weapon of mass destruction. Nobody is forced to eat all that junk, but people have no choice because only a small group can afford time and money associated with the good eating. That includes eating slowly. Most of my colleagues ate at their workplace in a hurry. They might as well drink cyanide in small doses.

Perseverance

This feature is by no means specific to America, but America is the only place where it is considered a must in every character. In fact, it is practically the only feature valued absolutely and without any amendments. Perseverance in trying to reach your goal, making the maximum effort again and again is praised as an utmost virtue. Whenever anyone is successful, he or she always mentions perseverance from childhood. This explains all the good things and bad things like relentless pursuit of justice and blind following of the rules, the stubbornness of the NRA and popularity of the books about the End of the World, Hef, Warren Buffet and Warren Beatty, Elliott Ness and Michael Corleone. Perseverance is not really a feature but rather a habit, and as any habit, it is in service of all the other qualities, whether good or bad. In the US, perseverance is so developed, that both good things and bad things go to their extremes.

In the words of Hal O'Leary:

I have never been goal oriented. It's like going through life with blinders, so focused that you miss all the opportunity in the periphery.

Very much so. We drift forward, not noticing that there is no water under the keel.

Money

Americans love money. There is only one true crime in this country and that is to be poor. When you are poor, everyone thinks there must be something wrong with you; like you have a mental deficiency of some sort. At the same time, if a person is rich, that person will be always called 'smart'. Not only professionals on retainer will say that, but also absolutely average people, strangers will say that. No wonder that the verb 'to make' as used in this country is a most popular expression like: 'make money' and 'make love'. In this country love of money is a legitimate character feature, same as kindness, malice, love or hate. Only in America you can see a genuine happiness on the face of the man who had just saved about $10. There was a poster in one of the hallways of my former job, 'Do you love money? Then we have something in common.'

Healthcare

In my opinion there's no healthcare in this country. Medical profession has been transformed into a money-laundering scheme. Physicians are not interested in making people healthy. Hippocratic Oath is dead, especially its main motto, "Do no harm." The non-existence of the healthcare as a universal right not only promotes the abuse but also connects it to the other abuses: health insurance, HMOs, prescription drug programs, Medicare and Medicaid, etc. Most of the health problems in this country are easily solvable but they are deliberately exaggerated and made worse, so that the vultures can benefit.

Family

Children are a precious commodity in this country. A single woman with children is a desirable partner for marriage, so is the single man with children. That's a terrific societal achievement. At the same time, an average American family is oriented towards disintegration. Children are not encouraged to live close to their parents after they become adults and parents are frequently put into nursing homes. I am not including here the minority families where things could be different. Some family ways seem very strange. It is common to give children drugs to control their behavior, to subject children to school punishments, to surrender children to the police. Teenagers are treated as time bombs, sexual perverts or potential drug addicts. Just check the price of the car insurance premiums for teenagers. In fact, it is very rare when the parents stay and fight for the rights of their children and if they do that, it is not really very much appreciated by the others especially if the children are in the age of elementary or middle school.

One of the most troubling issues is the issue of treating the young people, especially the ones in the military with praise. Jingoism, the unconditional 'support of our boys and girls' is pure hypocrisy and stupidity. It results in death. I can't judge the individuals but it is my opinion that there is something very wrong with the family morals in this area.

Smiles, Hugs, and Shoving

Americans smile even if they show you a middle finger. Whenever you meet an American unofficially he/she would smile to you, hug you at the shoulder, up close and personal. That's what we call a cultural difference; it seems uncomfortable to me to be hugged by someone I don't know well. As for the smiles, I prefer a smile for a reason. If a person smiles for no reason, I consider such person pretentious, unless he/ she is in love. Permanent smiling annoys. It denigrates human character and insults human intelligence. It is especially true when you see how quickly those smiles vanish when money comes into play.

Homemaking

You can only admire American tenacity and skills when they work on their homes. Most American dads are handymen. They can repair things, maintain machinery, remodel, and paint, mow the grass, and take care of all aspects of the property. Moms are economical, home-oriented and sweet. They smile a lot. They also take care of flowers, children, vegetables and dogs. Nearly every household has a pickup truck, always filled with wood or something else. Children are taught to take care of the property, to appreciate its value, etc.

The twist here is that about 70% of the property value is defined by its location. Also, most of the contemporary middle-class homes are houses of cards. A bare hand can smash through the internal drywall. It is very tough to really heat or cool such houses; that's why heating or electric bills are high. To maintain such house is a full-time job, which takes practically all the time of the average Joe/ Jane aside from actually working for living. That explains why people here are not very curious about much of anything or read literature. They are too tired.

Laws

Americans are proud of being a 'nation of laws'. What it means is that there are numerous petty laws that are oblivious of the general national character and customs. As a result, there are written laws for everything; from dressing right to dying right. People are desperately afraid of each other because a lawsuit is a way to get money. Criminal laws are so broad that jails are filled up to capacity all the time.

At the same time, this criminal justice system is the only one allowing deals, when the criminal actually can plead guilty to some charge and thus avoid penalty for a more serious one. Dealing in Justice? That's mind-boggling. Police brutality has become a normal thing. The horrible stench of manhunt is in the air and bounty hunters benefit.

As much as we admire our laws, we violate the laws of others. Most of our wars, starting with the extermination of the Indians, were blatant violations of laws, treaties and agreements. American government is perhaps the most consistent and persistent in exercising the treacherous foreign policy. The real reason for it is again that there is no such thing as an American society; thus the ruling group cannot rely on certain unwritten rules of conduct. Basically, the rulers can do what they wish. They can abuse the citizen who has no ability to strike back. None of the rulers, even those in jail for their behavior, will be ostracized by the society or even reprimanded in any societal way. There is no such thing as honor. It does not mean that there are no honorable people; there are many. But the society does not consider honor as a virtue. The cynical principle of American business"I am honest until proven otherwise," (attributed to John O'Hara) had replaced the noble one 'Honest work for Honest pay.'

Organization

Americans are very organized. It is a pleasure to watch a fire team, the police working in unison or the road workers. When I was in Florida I admired the preparations to hurricanes. Wherever Americans are, they bring with them the spirit of organization, structuring, efficiency and work done. It is only when something unusual happens, that the problems arise. Once I was in South Carolina and there was a small fire in the room over mine. When I came back from the meeting, I wanted to see if there was any damage in my room. The police didn't allow me to come up because they claimed that the firefighters were still there. The policeman was blocking the elevator door. I bypassed him, went to the second floor and called the elevator from there. Of course, there were no firefighters in the room and my things had some water damage. Go figure. The seemingly flawless logic of organized activities provides for the wrong sense of arrogance and self-righteousness. Americans frequently think that if they are organized and others are not, that means there is something wrong with those others and that has to be fixed. "What do we do with those people?" is heard frequently on TV, in Congress, and even at the family gatherings. This way of thinking is so embedded in the minds of the people that they never notice how strange it sounds and to what perils it might lead to.

Politics of Shorts

Russian men didn't wear shorts. Russian women didn't either, except maybe very young girls. That's how it was in my time. Americans wear shorts, overalls, strange flannel shirts, camouflage fatigues, dungarees, jeans, etc. All of that is practical, cheap and totally tasteless. Middle-aged men in shorts, women in spandexes, all of that would seem looking like it must be hereditary. The worst happens when some of those men suddenly come out in double–breasted suits or tuxedos and women-in gowns or cocktail-dresses. They look unnatural in those stylish garments.

Shorts and spandexes kill the proper step, the grace of walking. That's why women here don't walk properly. They either trot like little puppies or make strange movements as if they are hammering a nail every time they make a step. Men in shorts look like overgrown teenagers. About 40% of the men are overweight, but they still wear shorts and like to show themselves in public that way. People with childish mentality commit wars and destruction.

Groupthink

It is by no means an American phenomenon, but as there is no such thing as social character, 'groupthink' soars in the US. Every corporation has 'corpthink', GOP has 'Repthink' and Dems have 'Demthink.' Paradoxically, the groupthink is used as an excuse to avoid personal responsibilities for anything. In short, groupthink is a powerful tool for ignorance and its manifestation is a symptom of something very wrong happening inside the society. For a society built on the personal responsibility and accountability, groupthink undermines its cornerstones.

Personal

I don't know if there is a Utopia, but I am certain that we must act as though there can be...

Sean O'Leary

Wine to Blood

Fatigue

The sense of fatigue is overwhelming and permanent. It appeared in about six months after we came to this country and stays with me ever since. Sometimes, when I am alone, it takes over completely. It took me fiffteen years to figure out the reason. The reason is my internal, natural opposition to what I have to do every day. I do all the necessary things, play the life game, but I don't want to do it. Thus I have to control myself every step on the way and that is tiresome. Everything that I do in the external world I would prefer to do differently, in my own way, the way I understand. As I cannot do that my way, and being a rational being, I 'do as Romans do' but that does not make me happy and it slowly exhausts me. I relax sparingly when I read a book or talk to my family.

Education

I am the only person now in my family who never studied in this country. The great side of that is that the actual skills are still worth more in this country than the paperwork. The tough part is that I realize that the way the education system is structured here I might never have become a scientist.

I teach regularly in the university. I also watched how my son studied at school and university. The deregulated K-12 system in which schools are supported locally and rely on the property taxes, and the lack of national school standards result in the obvious fragmentation and broken glass system. No issue in this country is more discussed than education and no issue is so vulnerable to hypocrisy. In all those rants about 'no child left behind,' SAT and PSAT, the teenage problems persist. The real question is always avoided: why do we need K-12 schools? What can we expect from them? And the answer (at least as I see it) is NOTHING.

The primary function of education in every society is to raise a citizen. This function is removed from the process here and thus the schools are rendered ineffective. When local authorities exclude from the studies (not include, mind you) anything that contradicts with views and perceptions of the local majority, there can be no good education. We pay our teachers higher salaries, but they still are afraid of controversy. After all, they are responsible for the young minds. Once I taught in the Upward Bound Program in Ohio for the impoverished Appalachian kids. I was supposed to teach physics and math. It became clear to me that those kids were not only malnourished but totally deprived of simple attention; the TLC (tender loving care) that all children need. I said to their parents, "If you really want your child to know physics, get him a notebook and tell him to research and study your farming machinery for example. Let him find out how they work, what forces are there, why the fuel is needed, coolant, etc. Tell him to write it all in the notebook in such a way, that you will be able to understand. When he does that, he will know physics." They thought I was joking.

In the universities I discovered the same thing. The idea that you can study anything you like achieves nothing. The primary goal of the higher education is not to pass tests, but to develop an ability to acquire knowledge on your own with a systematic approach to everything. That cannot be achieved if the professors are so full of themselves that they seriously think that science begins with them. People have to understand that science, engineering, literature are not just static things. Like an ocean, they existed before and will exist after, and like an ocean they can be polluted; so we better be very careful because to pollute is much easier than to improve. Unfortunately, academia treats knowledge like some kind of a commodity where the bottom-line rules. There are thousands of unnecessary courses and teaching staff lacks professionalism, to say the least. It results in the mass production of the 'homo ignoramus,' the totally ignorant, who think he is very knowledgeable. You can see the results in our political leadership. Their self-control mechanism has been replaced simply by the adherence to the majority. In engineering it manifests in an abundance of young people who blindly believe that they possess knowledge without even trying to look around. They are conformists.

Friendship

I consider friendship a sacrosanct feeling, second only to love. As such I never expected to have many friends in this life. I lost most of my friends on the other side forever. Here it is very difficult to maintain such friendship because it can only develop with mutual respect and respect is not something appreciated here. I have many nice people around; we talk to them, keep in touch, etc., but I would never trust my child to their keeping, neither would I trust them with my money or my welfare. As I specified above, there is no such thing as honor here and thus I cannot trust people here. I just do not know; they might be OK and they might not. I would make a comparison with the ideal gas models or pool balls. We can easily find each other and collide; there is inertia of the movement, but there is no intermolecular potential or cohesion, so to speak. This is OK, but is it friendship? Thus, the best way here is not to expect very much and not to promise very much.

Diversity

People from Caucasus would be very much annoyed if they find out that all those whitey WASPS call themselves Caucasians. In fact I wonder if any of the Americans know that the racial traits such as Latinos, Blacks, Caucasians, Asians and Middle-Easterners are based on the old, totally flawed, racist theories and gradations, which had been subsequently totally discredited by modern anthropology. There is no such thing as a Caucasian ethnicity or race. There are no blacks because there are at least six or seven distinct African races from Hottentots to Bantu. There are no 'Middle-Eastern people'. Actually, the so-called WASPS are predominantly of Swedish-German origins and those are well –known by reputation as the 'dullest and most limited people in Europe'☺ That's how they are described in classic Western European literature.

I think that we in this country deliberately try to disconnect people by emphasizing the differences instead of promoting the similarities. We should show again and again how close the cultures are, how easy it is to absorb the best in others, how insignificant are the petty differences. The primary necessity for acknowledging a connection is respect which, of course, does not exist in this society. It is that simple.

Spiritual life

I am not a religious man. At the same time, I was brought up to respect any true religion that acknowledges achievements by truly religious people standing firm for their beliefs and also at the same time being humble and selfless in the face of their "Higher Being.," Whatever it is, I always associate it with commitment. It totally lacks hypocrisy and strives for virtue and wisdom. Bottom line, it is tough to be truly religious and tough it should be.

In this country, this criterion does not work. I would even dare to say that I think that most of the people here, except maybe Buddhists and Irish Catholics are not really religious. They go to churches, pray, read the Bible and hold hands at dinners, but for them God is like a benevolent uncle, who is always kind to them. They assume that He lives here in America. Someone even called this country the God's realm. From the point of view of true religion such views are paganism. The US middle class does not own God. In fact, He owns everything and everyone. So I feel very uneasy sometimes when I hear the televangelists vehemently proclaiming that they speak to God and know His wishes. That is sacrilege and we can be punished for it.

As for myself I do believe that God knows better (if He exists) and when my time comes, He will be just. Gods are just, right?

Work

I work as an engineer. The engineering legacy of the US is outstanding. It stands on the works of such giants and Edison and Robert Wood, Rieblings, Fulton and Eriksson, Wright brothers, Edison, Tesla, Charles Ellis, Henry Ford and many others. It is primarily an applied skill, but what a beautiful skill! The achievements are enormous; from the Brooklyn Bridge to the Space Shuttle. The US school of engineering is by far the most knowledgeable. The engineering profession is extremely rewarding and self-sufficient. Due to the licensing process experienced professionals can go into business for themselves, do consulting, etc. The pay is still pretty good. At the same time I need to mention an extreme conservatism of the engineering profession in the sense of being prone to standard solutions, lack of creativity and certain limits of imagination. I would argue that those advanced features are not cultivated in our engineering schools. Also I need to state that the hiring and firing at will doesn't benefit the best people. A person has to cultivate connections more and more, and that interferes with the normal working process. Not the best are hired, but those most convenient and those most prone to conformity in many cases. That's especially hard for young people.

Lost and Found

I lost my handwriting. Computers and ball-point pens killed it. I still struggle to maintain my reading skills despite the computers. It is an ugly secret that computers actully reduce reading skills and make people less knowledgeable. I do my best to fight it.

I lost my sense of the female mystery. There are so many woman's magazines, so many nude bodies, so many TV shows like Sex and the City, so many gynecologists, sex pathologists, etc. The sanctity, the thrill of a relationship is permanently damaged and only old books are the cure.

I lost the feel of happiness. The old criteria are gone, replaced by new ones I don't believe in. Whatever I do, does not thrill me anymore. Only family successes still make me happy for a while.

What I gained were new impressions of different places and people. America, France, Italy, Spain, Portugal. I would never have encountered new people, with new faces, and new languages. I loved that dearly. It helped me in my work.

What am I?

Many immigrants and very prominent ones asked themselves the same question. Lion Feuchtwanger said once," I live in the US. My native language is German. My soul is Jewish." I will try to something similar, "I live in the US. I am of Russian-Jewish descent. Always wanted to be Irish." I think, my Irish soul somehow lost its way and landed at the Russian borders where it engaged in drinking and learning Russian poetry until the time came to go back. I am still on the journey if I may say.

On Immigration

Immigration is an escape. No one in his or her right mind would want to leave their native country for good, especially if there's a big chance of never coming back. People run away. The experience of running away from your own kind is devastating forever. Thus personal happiness is gone and the only possible equivalent would be the happiness of children. We live for them. Our primary goal is for them never to experience fear and have to run. We have a responsibility to watch and preserve all freedom-supporting institutions in the country even if it means to leap over the precipice like Aesop. Our children have to be alive, liberated and free to choose. There is no other goal.

Conclusion: we are here as sentinels

I would like to state that whatever I said about this country and its people is not meant as negative. This country is not wonderful or perfect and neither are other countries. I live here. It means that negative and positive things here are mine to share. This is my place; I will live the rest of my life and die here. Thus I take everything I can and offer a lot in return. At the same time my words represent my honest and direct opinion, and as a man of experience I have a right to state it. As one Russian poet said, "My people are not complete without me." That is we all are valuable. One of the oldest stereotypical beliefs is that the first generation immigrants are the undesirables. Literature and entertainment are full of characters portraying us like living ghosts, unable to change and embrace the new life. That is not true. We are a part of the people here and we are here to help. We have our personalities; we don't have to change who we are. We will not be ignored or discarded. Neither are we expendable. We are the sentinels, watchers. Our experience is unique and if it taught us anything-it is how to expose the symptoms of the creepy evil and oppression emerging from anywhere and under any pretense in our society. We, by definition, are those canaries who sense the smell of gas long before it fills the mine and explodes. In the same way, our voice, though critical, is always well-intentioned.

I earned my right to fulfill these functions to the best of my abilities and I will exercise those rights whenever I deem it necessary. That's my responsibility to freedom and my duty as a citizen, as a father and as a husband.

Chapter 3

Darkness

There are two kinds of light—
the glow that illuminates and
the glare that obscures...

J. Thurber

Темнота

Мы никогда не смотрим в темноту,
Когда на сцене роль свою играем,
И душу нараспашку открываем,
Под блестками скрывая наготу,

Когда же к нам приходит темнота,
Сжимаемся от холода и страха.
То злая нам мерещится собака,
То гробового свода глухота.

И стужа нас преследует везде,
В тропическом лесу как на Аляске,
Скрипят морозно старые салазки
По неизменной вечной мерзлоте.

Мы вышли все из тьмы и пустоты,
Театр теней плясал на голой стенке,
И в отраженном пламени горелки
То зубы проявлялись, то хвосты.

И все казалось, свет поможет нам
Увидеть ясно все дела людские,
Но чудища страшнее чем морские
По освещенным прятались углам.

Поэтому мне темень по душе,
А лучше всех-закаты и рассветы,
Осенние, бессонные приметы,
Безмолвной тайной ходят в камыше.

Всем блеском мудреца не проведешь.
Светильники картину искажают.
Лишь тишина все тайны раскрывает.
Ее без темноты не обретешь.

IN LIGHT OR DARKNESS

Whenever I appear upon a stage,
And bear the glare of public scrutiny,
The sudden wish for darkness rules supreme.
The sense is that I stand in nudity.

With darkness though, I shiver from the cold,
The kind that musty coffins might suggest
And with it all the ogres one might fear
Appear in nightmares devils never guessed.

The cold with darkness will not go away.
Alaska cannot match it for degree.
And these will make us seek both heat and light,
But neither is desired, it's plain to see.

It seems we have an option, hot or cold,
(O'er sand or permafrost our sledges screech)
Will it be dark or light, a bitter choice,
And lost is solace that we cannot reach.

In light, I thought the dark will soothe the soul,
But there, I found the horror only grew
In dark, I thought the light would show the way
Yet beasties from the lighted corners flew.

But lo, between the darkness and the glare,
And falling soft like dew upon the lawn,
I find at last, in solace andin peace,
A soothing twilight with its dusk and dawn.

It is because I know that wisdom seeks
A truth that neither light or dark provide.
A soothing subtle truth that softly speaks
To things that light or darkness tend to hide.

When you are at sea at night you feel the ocean breathing heavily but you see absolutely nothing and that's scary. The greatness of Nature, the power of waves and your own humility are there to clear your mind from the stroboscopic glare of the TV-images.

When looking at those images, your eyes get used to the fragmentation; you get tired easily and dose off. Everything drowns in the glare: unnaturally skinny, naked women, violence, death, sex, courtroom dramas, Dracula, UFOs, political corruption and wars. The glare prevents us from thinking and obscures the real things in life. That's when monsters come out. They are the products of the sleeping mind as in the *Los Caprices* by F. Goya; ugly, evil, ever-dominating, malicious ghouls. When the TV volume is turned off, the people's behavior becomes grotesque; noise is everything, sense is nothing. Even God becomes a source of noise: God, God, God pounds you. Which God, where? How is God connected to the man in a blue suite on the TV podium? All religions in the world emphasize meditation and restraint. Noise is not a part of God's Providence. Isn't silence still golden? Wasn't it that once darkness and silence ruled the Earth when only the Holy Spirit glided over the waters?

The profound influence of darkness is depicted in the movie *Dancing With Wolves*, about a Union officer alone, on the Texas frontier. He was a man of war, a man of quick decisions and short thinking. He never pondered on what was under his feet or looked up at the stars. Life on the frontier, dark solitude, close encounters with Nature prepared him for the new experience of cooperating with the Indians. If he was with his regiment, his comrades-in arms, vulgar men with the killer instinct, he would be distracted by the glare; by the smell of war, by the difference in color of the people, by fear, by ignorance, by all those monsters who reside in the stroboscopic light. But he was alone. Darkness and silence fell upon him. That sharpened his feelings, promoted goodness and suppressed the beast in him. Thus the Indians gave him an Indian name as they would call one of their own. He stopped being Paleface and became Dancing With Wolves. It was like a baptism; he became a better man. From that moment his choice was clear and noble In a way, through the encounter with Indians, he understood and defeated his own savagery, became self–aware as a true Christian should be.

This rare uplifting feeling I experienced myself when I was leaving Russia for good and the only music remaining in me since then is the Marché, "Farewell of the Slavic Woman." I play it every day in my car and it doesn't sound right. It's a railway departure march and it needs an orchestra in the open air to sound properly. My old country was a railway world. The first sound I remember from my childhood is the train whistle. Nobody played that Marché at the station on the day of our departure and there were no crying women or soldiers waving hands through the doors. The evening was cold and we were standing under the shadow of the overpass in a frozen silence. Mist crawled from beneath the train, red and black from the sparks and coal-fed heaters of the carriages. It enveloped us, took us in and pushed us towards the river as if not just the train but the whole platform was on the way to the great bridge, the only one leading to the country capital, to the airport, to the gate abroad, out, away, forever.

People hovered in the mist, angry, tired and scared. The bell chimed and the radio voice announced arrivals and departures. Whispering started to fade as the people boarded the train, and when the doors closed it was only darkness with rain and distorted faces glued to the greasy windows. Then the music started somewhere inside the train; one of the passengers was playing an accordion. The train slowly pulled away from the platform, and while it was making its way through the station district and further on through the surrounding woods. The bridge appeared in front of us as a mechanical mass of inevitability, and music still sounded following the beat of the wheels. After we crossed the bridge the lights dimmed and the Farewell Marché subsided.

Then again we were standing in the lighted circle in the middle of the dark airport hall and the customs people were rummaging through our things. No money or documents were allowed except for the private jewelry like wedding rings and earrings. I had a suitcase full of books, with permission. The officers looked through each of the books page by page, slowly, methodically with the persistence of the mentally disturbed. They didn't say anything. We weren't worthy because weeks ago we surrendered our passports and other IDs, and became invisible. The crowd watched us from the dark and eyes of the people glimmered as if the hall was filled with wild animals.

There was a time when that hall hosted privileged foreigners. Some of the sofas still stood there, ragged, with remnants of expensive upholstery hanging from the sides. People didn't sit on them anymore; the sofas were buried under mountains of suitcases. Several hundred people packed in that hall; silent, secretive, whispering in the dark. Whispers rustled through the air, bounced at the walls hitting each other, reaching us in fragments. Ethnic Germans were leaving after 500 years of residency and their ancient, archaic speech filled the space with gothic feeling. The government of Germany delayed their entrance visas, and they had been waiting for weeks, patiently, quietly, with that eternal dignity, they had retained through hundreds of years. Everyone was neatly dressed, men were shaved, and all the children were attended to. They waited the same way they tilled their soil every spring, awaiting for the mystery of a harvest. Maybe it will come and maybe will not; all is in God's hands.

When we passed the last checkpoint, I looked back through the glass wall. A tall, blond woman dressed in a long, smooth dress with ethnic embroidery was standing on the other side looking straight at me. She seemed distracted; her glance was unfocused, directed somewhere through the airfield, towards the border far away, that invisible line on the other side of which was rest, clean linen, a warm bed, and a life of hope. In about two hours we would cross that border the way birds cross it every season, knowing that they will return. Only we will not return.

She smiled at me and blew us all a kiss. At that very moment, I heard that music again, that powerful and tender Marché that would stay with me through the years of exile. The glare subsided and the illumination sparkled at the end of the terminal tunnel. The dawn was coming.

We all have darkness in our souls. It can become a source of the redeeming inner light if only we agree to the twilight and music in it.

Image By
Andrea Izzotti
ID:416978029

Chapter 4

Strange Things

When power corrupts, poetry cleanses..

John F. Kennedy

На Могиле Апполинера

Хотел бы иметь я в доме своем,
Жену, наделенную трезвым умом...

(Г. Апполинер)

I would like to have a wife with sober wisdom in my home

(G. Apollinaire)

Благословляю того, кто придумал газ в квартирах.....

(М, Булгаков. Из переписки)

(I bless those who invented the gas in the apartments. M Bulgakov)

Хотел бы иметь я в доме своем....
Но дома пока не имею,
И кошку с веселым. пушистым хвостом
Не скоро еще я пригрею,

Простые желанья сложнее всего,
Истории странная правда,
Захочешь как-будто всего-ничего.
И жизнью пожертвовать надо.

Как странно устроен наш мир, господа
Художники, барды, поэты
Мечтают немножко пожить для себя,
Но роскоши этой им нету.

Отмечены щедрой рукою судьбы
Все яблоки райского сада
Невеждам, а умным отвеку даны,
Лишь корка, да кисть винограда.

Ваганты, сказители, люди дорог,
И просто свободные души,
Отмечены с детства ступить за порог
С извечной надеждой на случай,

Что кончится путь и наступит покой,
Сирень заплетет подоконник,
И разумом трезвой подруге родной
Он будет начитывать сонник.

Но так не бывает, хотел, не хотел,
Гийом, Михаил, все едино,
Не богом, а чертом отмечен предел
Усилиям блудного сына.

Из серого камня надгробье стоит
Тому, кто желал так немного.
И где-то под огненным солнцем лежит
Последняя наша дорога.

At the Apollinaire's Tomb

A house, a furry cat that they might tease
A home for them, but can it ever be,
Or are they those the fates refuse to please,
Ignoring with disdain their humble plea?

It's strange, but simple comforts others gain
Become complex for them and are denied.
But, thus the vagrant poets must remain,
True to the cause for which they lived and died.

It's those who give the most who reap the least
The sacrifice they make we rarely note.
In making sure that we won't miss the feast,
We've little time for what the poet wrote.

It seems that fate has constantly reserved
The best that could be found in nature's spread
For just the very ones that least deserved,
While for the poets meager grapes and bread.

Those vagrants, whose demands were not extreme,
Sought little, but the end was never kind
The lilac covered walls were just a dream.
The loving wife who read, they could not find.

For you, Bulgakov and Apollinaire,
The Devil has defined you, not a God.
No matter that your gifts to us are rare
Our gifts to you were naught but stone and sod.

The gray stones match a solemn overcast
But then a sudden ray of sun lays bare
The promise that the darkness may not last,
If only we who follow show we care.

When Robert Burns' mother saw a stone monument on his tomb, she lamented, "Oh, Robbie, you asked people for bread and you received a stone." Such fate is common for many poets. Many of them are buried at the Per La Chaise cemetery in Paris, Gilliam Apollinaire among them. He was a poet and a novelist, a true follower of Francois Villon, the legendary troubadour of the medieval France who mysteriously vanished in the 14th Century. In his novel *A Poet Murdered,* Apollinaire fantasized about a society in which poets were killed and persecuted for 'being of no use." The most merciless persecutions in the novel happened in the USA. Apollinaire lived a life of a nomad, was denied a French citizenship for a long time, went to WWI and was severely wounded. He never fully recovered and died from the Spanish Flu in 1918. He received his citizenship only during the war. Despite immense popularity and personal bravery his private life was miserable and he suffered from deep depression. In Russia, writer Michael Bulgakov lived in poverty and misery all his life. He wrote immortal novels like "Maestro and Margarita" but could never visit his younger brother in Paris because of the travel restrictions imposed by Stalin's regime. His plays were forbidden, his literary works weren't printed and the official state media slandered him. He couldn't secure employment, suffered from a debilitating disease and died while fairly young.

Anna Akhmatova, the Taormina Poet Laureate, never had a decent lodging. Her first husband was executed by the Russian Secret Police, her third husband shared the same fate, her son was imprisoned for a long time, and most of her friends shared the similar fate. She herself was shunned by the political elite, slandered in the state media and denied even the basic necessities. She died in obscurity.

Somehow for a poet to desire the simple comforts of life, like shelter, adequate food, hot water, gas, etc. seems to be out of reach. It's as if fate denies them peace of mind. Edgar Allan Poe died young and in misery but there is a huge stone on his tomb. Constantine Balmont, the famous Russian poet, translated Poe's poems and speculated that the tombstone was there, "to prevent the escape of the powerful Poe's spirit." When you visit an ancient cemetery, look for the great poets, overturn their tombstones and let the spirits go free.

Image By
Komkrit Preechachanwate
ID:599536928

Chapter 5

At The Wall

Time and again foul things attacked me...

Beowulf
Translated by S. Heaney

У СТЕНЫ

Смиренное кладбище Пер-Лашез,
За все мои скитания подарок.
Вот здесь могила Вальдека Роше,
А там-стена с тенями коммунаров.

Аллея коммунистов в чистоте
Содержится, могилы все в порядке.
Стена стоит в спокойной наготе,
Полоски, как на старенькой терадке.

Не видно ни следа от той весны,
Когда на улицах гремели пушки.
И если тени бродят у стены,
То и они уже давно старушки.

Убытки за последние сто лет
На косточках подсчитаны и счеты
Подведены, партийный комитет
Направлен на подземные работы.

Но тени просят у меня ключи
К загадке до сих пор непостижимой,
На месте, где стояли палачи,
Отведены наследникам могилы.

Необходимо все им обьяснить,
Все рассказать за этот миг короткий,
Поймать времен связующую нить,
Но вновь блестят старинные винтовки.

Мне остается только рядом встать
В дыму навстречу новым постояльцам..
Успеть бы хоть рукою указать
На звездочки в фуражках у версальцев.

WITH MY SON AT THE WALL OF COMMUNARS AT PERE LA CHAISE CEMETERY

I stand beside my son at Pere Lachaise
The Wall of Communards recalls the plight
Of communists who faced the Versailles troops
And died for freedom as a human right.

And now we see their shadows gather there.
As if to summon us to join the cause,
A cause that we cannot allow to die.
The danger that we might, must give us pause.

The human bones as on an abacus
Record betrayal hard to understand
The underground Committees plot their guile
As comrades hailing from a common land.

The stars found on the caps of Versailliers.
The star the Party faithful must obey.
"From history, not ashes but the fire."
And Jean Joures shows us a way.
But as I ponder this, there's something strange
No longer is the horror just recall.
I find the past and present now as one.
My son, moves to the shadows at the wall.

He stands his ground beside the Communards,
While here among the Versailliers am I
They raise their shinning rifles to take aim,
And frantically I reach and with a cry,

I plead and call for him to come away.
So young, he must not be allowed to die,
But should he not, as they, observe the day?
But heart to heart, the question must be, Why?.

And as I look, Behold, a subtle smile
Has crossed his face, and suddenly, I'm swept
Into a frantic urge to stand with him
Beside the Communards for whom we wept.

"Eternal struggle" oaths are needed now
To take it on with courage and with pride.
No less than an epiphany for me,
I move to take my place now at his side.

The Pere La Chaise cemetery in Paris. is a very ancient place; many famous people are buried there. Frederick Chopin is buried there, along with Balzac and Edith Piaf, 'The Sparrow of Paris'. We have many great country singers in the US, but in all honesty, can we call anyone of them a Sparrow or a Nightingale?

There is a Wall of Communards and an alley in front of it where prominent French Communists are buried. The Communards were the people who fought for the Paris Commune in 1871. It is an old story. They ruled Paris for about two months, trying to restore some order during the disastrous war with Prussia. Eventually they were overrun by the forces of the conservative government in Versailles. It was a bloody massacre. Cannons were used to shoot at the crowds of civilians; thousands were executed, including women and children. The last Communards made their stand at the wall at the Per La Chaise cemetery. They were all shot dead. The executioners were standing right along the alley where now the French Communists rest in peace.

Communards were idealists. They proclaimed a new society, a society of true equality. Their descendants in the twentieth century took power in Russia and other countries and embarked on a mission to make people happy. Eighty years later and millions people fewer the anomaly died. It is not that Humanity proved unworthy. It is just that it happens that the perception of happiness is different for different people and there is no such thing as universal satisfaction. Unless you want to kill all the people, you have to acknowledge the simple truth that we are all as different spiritually as we are similar physically.

French Communist Party was loyal to the ideological leadership and for a long period of time it did not recognize Stalin's terror even though he betrayed the revolutionary principles and massacred everyone who challenged his absolute power. They were good people. Many of them were active in the Resistance and by far the French Communists sacrificed the most in that struggle. And still, for a long time they refused to acknowledge Stalin's terror and betrayal, or his destruction of the revolutionary spirit.

It was rainy and misty. My son wanted to know everything about the place. After I told him the story he approached to the Wall and stood there for some time. For a brief moment the shadows at the wall came back to life. There they were standing, the ragged knights of elusive hope, surrounding my son, while the Versailles forces around me were rising their rifles. My son was smiling. I was helpless to warn him, to take his hand and draw him away. All I could do was to step forward and join him, so that we both could see the little red stars on the soldiers' *caskettes*. It was a moment of transfiguration and closure of the full circle.

Jean Joures said, "We want to take from the past history not ashes, but fire." Yes, and in the end the idealists are executed by any power, right or left. But the fire remains the eternal one, and the person who has a gift to see it should be happy to burn with it.

Image By
Breakermaximus
ID: 223093090

Chapter 6

Martyrs

What you don't understand, you can't possess..

Johan Wolfgang Goethe

ПАРАПСИХОЛОГИЯ

В Париже,
На Еврейском острове есть табличка о том,
что в 1308 году там был сожжен
Жак Моле,
последний Великий Магистр Ордена Тамплиеров.

In Paris, on the Jewish Island, the Île aux Juifs
there's a memorial desk that in 1314, Jacques de Molay,
the last Grandmaster of the Knights Templar was burned alive there..

Когда меня сжигали на костре,
На острове Еврейском поздно ночью,
Я обещал ликующей толпе,
Что я вернусь увидеть все воочью.

Я обещал всем этим королям,
Что мир изменится неузнаваем
И дым костров под сенью Нотр-Дам
Потомкам будет представляться раем.

Я говорил пророчества свои,
Пока душа моя не отлетела,
Блуждать по дальним уголкам Земли,
Не зная ни покоя ни предела.

За горькое проклятье палачам
За рыцарское гордое упрямство
Мне вечное скитанье даровал,
Тот, кто создал и время и пространство.

Дано мне было в жизни суете
Объединяться с душами младенцев,
Кто весь свой век проводит в наготе,
Еретиков, поэтов, отщепенцев.

Они мне объяснили весь поток
Событий действий, чувств невыразимых.
И я давно уж больше не пророк,
Лишь ученик неправедно гонимых.

Я вспоминаю рыцарство свое
С улыбкой все познавшего на свете.
Как мало знали мы про бытие,
Какие мы тогда все были дети.

Теперь, когда встаю я на костер
С очередным еретиком прощаясь,
Я с ним веду последний разговор
И мудростью его обогащаюсь.

Ему же я стараюсь передать
Мою отвагу и мою свободу.
В надежде, что постигнет благодать
Кому хватало в жизни лишь на воду.

И вновь в толпе при виде мудреца,
Я праздник духа с радостью предвижу
До огненного нашего конца
На незаметном острове в Париже.

Paranormal

When at the stake they burned me late at night,
I swore to all the crowd I would return.
I also promised all the Kings of fame,
That times would surely change, and they would learn

The smoke above the shades of Notre-Dame,
Would bring descendants little but delight.
For all the wisdom I had prophesied,
Before the earthbound body freed my soul
To wander limitless the world round,

Sans any peace or promise of parole,
And no repose or silence to be found,
With certainty, would now be certified.

He, who created endless time and space,
Had, for my curse of executioners
And for my Knightly pride and stubbornness,
All traits that he admittedly prefers,
With liberality and yes, largess,
He granted me this freedom with all grace.

As such, I could unite with kindred souls,
Who thus, like naked babes, are satisfied
To spend their lonely lives in solitude
With heretics and poets; those denied
The panoramas others may have viewed;
The modern life and choice of other goals.

They had explained to me the ebb and flow
Of actions and events beyond the pale,
And since then, I'm no prophet anymore,
But student of the persecuted frail,
The ones with whom I had a strong rapport;
The ones to whom so very much I owe.

So now as I look back on my Knighthood,
With greater knowledge and with sympathy,
I realize how little then we knew
Of what it meant to know that one is free,
Or what of life, we didn't have a clue;
So many things we never understood.

And now, when I stand up to face the fire
To bid farewell to heretic and bard,
It's not my place to prophecy and boast,
For now, humility can make it hard
To find an answer or a quick riposte;
For wisdom, it's my place to just inquire.

But then there's spirit and veracity,
A truth that only free Knights can possess,
To be delivered by a grace divine
To those who in this life will know distress,
Who slates their thirst with brine, denied the wine;
The ones we never find in history.

But then I look about, and I can see
A Knight like me, with courage in his heart;
A Knight like me refusing to be cowed;
A Knight like me who proudly stands apart.
He'll face the fiery end with head unbowed
On this small island, here in old Paris.

Philippe Le Belle (The Handsome) was a ruthless King of France in the fourteenth century. To fortify his absolute power he falsely accused the powerful Templar Knights of treason, sorcery and heresy. After horrible tortures hundreds were executed. In 1314 on the Jewish Island in Paris Jacques de Molay, the last Great Magistrate of the Templars was burned alive. He was a very brave man. Already being engulfed in flames, he cursed King Philippe and his accomplices and predicted that they all would pay for their crime. After the flame subsided the black charred hand still threatened the people. King Philippe died soon after. His three sons died very quickly one-by–one and the dynasty was lost. The curse brought the 100 years' War and only the counter-sacrifice, the great injustice of the burning of Joan of Arc exonerated France from it.

When I visited the island, I imagined that the powerful spirit of Jacques de Molay received a gift from God to wonder endlessly and meet other heretics that were wise and compassionate people. That would be a marvelous experience, when the wizards would enrich him with their love of humanity and he would give them his strength, valor and eternal strife for freedom.

We still burn our heretics at stake. But didn't you notice that they always come back, stronger, more resilient, ready for the new battles? When we burned our black people at the Lynch trials, thousands of black charred hands cursed us forever and new, more courageous people took their place. I believe that each of those people had the heart of a Templar Knight. The question is whether this horrible multiple curse is still upon us or not. What do you think?

Image By
Issara Anujun
ID: 585616094

Chapter 7

Transformations

The Red Queen shook her head. "You may call it nonsense if you like," she said, " but I've heard nonsense be as sensible as a dictionary."

Lewis Carroll
Through the Looking-Glass

РАЗГОВОР

Как верится в бессмерти е души!
Не так, чтобы столы вертеть в Сочельник,
А так, чтобы проснуться в понедельник,
Среди пустыни, в каменной глуши.

Еще вчера сидел ты за столом,
А ныне под неопалимым солнцем,
Ты бредишь освежающим колодцем,
С очередным встречаясь миражом.

Ты веришь ли в переселенье душ?
Что вот ты вдруг свои часы проверил,
Как будто кто-то срок тебе отмерил,
А на параде все играют туш...

Как у Рабле замерзшие слова,
Оттаивают души от погоды.
И в теплом придыхании природы
Очередная пишется глава.

Чужая жизнь становится твоей,
Кружится голова от обретенья.
Ты позже ощутишь, что нет спасенья,
Как в воду погружаясь в мир теней.

Так правильней ли было бы сказать,
Что наш покой иллюзии подобен,
Никто не может вечно быть свободен,
И приговором душ пренебрегать.

Мы безотчетно думаем о них
И за угол посматриваем часто
Но наша настороженность напрасна,
Не уловить преображенья миг.

Поэтому мы молимся в церквях,
Неутомимо столики вращаем,
Вампиров потихоньку привечаем,
И книжки ужасов читаем при свечах.

A Discussion

So sorry that the lesser ones will pray,
Or otherwise seek peace in the occult.
In doing so, their reason must give way,
And life with little meaning will result.
Immortal is the soul, I do believe.
But turning of the tables, I'll forego,
Preferring just to wake up and receive
Whatever fate prepares both joy and woe.

I may have just been feasting yesterday
But now it's desert sands, unending sun,
Mirages that will sweep my mind away.
I may be at a loss but not undone.

While others still parade as music plays,
I welcome other souls, they do change hosts?
Unsure, I check my watch. I'm in a haze,
And I'm possessed by those, that some call ghosts?

I've often heard that frozen souls may thaw,
In ways that Rabelais notes words can do.
In trust that this be true, I stand in awe,
Confused with what I have become or who.

Surrounded now by souls becoming mine,
A sea of shadows ever-changing shape.
Whatever this may be, I can't define.
Possessed I am and there is no escape

I'm captured with no thought of peace of mind,
Like freedom it's at best, illusory.
And suddenly my life is redesigned.
I must obey, the souls have sentenced me.

So fleetingly they come, it's like a game.
I try, at times, to catch them with a glance.
But dancing like the flickering of a flame
They're here and gone. There is but little chance.

So sorry that the lesser ones will pray,
Or otherwise seek peace in the occult.
In doing so, their reason must give way,
And life with little meaning will result.

Ah, those movies! The Poltergeist, the Amityville Horror, the Halloween 1,2,3,4 Patrick Swayze as Ghost, Leslie Nielsen as Dracula, Denzel Washington in *The Fallen*.. There is always an evil spirit invading someone's body, roaming around; unsettled, unhappy and malicious. There are so many concepts. Do you know that in the Hindu religion, after you die, you are resurrected into another creature, human or animal? Russian poet Vysotsky joked once, that whatever you did in your first life would be reflected in the second. If you were a nice person, you become somebody or something nice again, like a dog or a horse. But the pig you were before, the pig you will be, that is certain.

The idea of spirits wondering among us is ancient. It appeals to our sense of humanity, the natural perception that something should remain of those deceased, some *aentelephia,* or energy of mind, a soul. So, it is very possible, that a foreign possession can take place. It can happen naturally, just walking down the street. The two worlds become one, intertwined, as in Love. There is no malice, just symbiosis, a necessity or a connection. We don't die. Instead we join a spiritual domain from which we are watched and wept for because of our negligence, stupidity and cruelty to each other, because we fear each other and renounce love. Meanwhile, we turn to the occult looking for clues to our strange feelings.

Immigration is very much like that, a metamorphosis. Goethe called it "Death for a new life." It's as if everything suddenly disappears and even the air is different. And for a long period of time you recognize people on the streets as if the spirits from your past had crossed the ocean with you. But eventually you find new spirits in the new place. They come to you and you befriend them. In the final dance, we all are together in a never-ending circle. No need for the occult.

Image By
Amanda Carden
ID: 345470666

Chapter 8

Psychology

A real book is not one that we read but one that reads us

W.H. Auden

ДИКАЯ СОБАКА ДИНГО

"Романы из школьной программы...."
Б. Слуцкий

Novels from the school time.
B. Slutsky

Тогда это было внеклассное чтенье,
Как будто весь зал отдан мне в попеченье,
Тяжелые полки, картонные лодки
Комоды, проходы, закладки, колодки.

И вечер тот темный со снегом каленым,
За окнами старого Дома Ученых,
Казался мне солнечным днем на Итаке,
От тоненькой книжки о дикой собаке.

И все очень просто, и все неспокойно,
И все относительно, зыбко, привольно.
Но радости веришь и горю внимаешь,
Как мягкому знаку во слове "товарищ."

Здесь непостижимым прозреньем пророка
Подсмотрен момент наступления срока,
Когда человеком становится глина,
И целое там, где была половина.

И все эти свечки, снега и заносы,
Все рыбки, страданья, конфеты и слезы,
Последние проблески детского счастья,
В преддверии жизни в борьбе и ненастье.

Рождение личности-невероятно,
Его откровенье звучит так невнятно,
Что автор, сумевший все это увидеть,
Стесняется Божье Мгновенье обидеть.

Но это неважно, великие цели
Нам дарят места в мировой карусели.
И лучиком светлым сияет во мраке
Короткая повесть о дикой собаке.

ASSIGNED READING

Assigned reading aside from class,
The library, as if it were mine alone
Row upon row of books,
Spaced by relics of another age.

Outside a darkened winter's night,
Falling snow, it seemed in globs
But here, the joy of a sunny day,
Lost in The Wild Dog Dingo.

The book presents a simple theme,
But none-the-less disturbing.
Feeling free, but yes, uncertain.
Where-in both joy and grief entwine.

The author snares but in a flash
The person fully formed,
A mosaic from the fragments
Of both childhood joys
And adolescent discontent.

A moment so sublime
Reserved for just one's self.
That the author fears rebuke
Should he sully the intent of God.

Great goals in life require a stretch
To snatch the carrousel's gold ring.
And the Wild Dog Dingo novel,
Shines like a sun ray through the dark.

A Matter of Character

When you work as an Aerospace Engineer for years it takes a toll on you. Life becomes boring and repetitious. Once I picked up an issue of National Geographic in the canteen and was stunned to see on the cover the photo of an African Masaya girl who appeared to be twelve to fourteen years old. It was like a spark in the darkness. I looked around at my fellow engineers and none of them had that visible, bright, overwhelming manifestation of a distinct character. She was a person fully aware of herself. Her dignity was as natural a part of her as the Masaya spear she held. I pinned that photo on the bulletin board in front of me and for years that girl's noble features greeted me every morning. I always felt inspired when looking at her. The photo remained there for at least a decade. Once a grey-haired veteran engineer stopped to ask about it.

"Excuse me, but who is that girl?
"She has quite a face," I said.
The man looked again, first at her, then at me.
"Yes," he said. "She has quite a face. I haven't seen many faces like that lately."

The character and proper transformation from adolescence to adulthood, so vivid in that girl's face had been the primary quest of many great artists and writers, from Tolstoy to Philip Roth. The study of that transformation is prevalent in both Russia and America with two literary works separated by nearly two decades and two devastating wars—*The Wild Dog Dingo* by Rouvim Fraerman (1939), and *The Catcher In The Rye* by JD Salinger (1951). The characters they draw are illuminating.

The Wild Dog Dingo was designated as an assigned summer reading for the teenagers. I read it, when I was but fourteen and I didn't like it. It was painful to read. Forty-two years later, when I learned that the people described in the book had all perished in the war, I realized that the book was never meant for teenagers. It was a book of true love. Tanya Sabaneeva, the female protagonist in The *Wild Dog* turned fifteen in 1939. Stalin was in power and life was cheap. People of the arts were praising him for his 'honesty and wisdom.' From dusk till dawn that monotonic acclaim came from every radio. The book though, was not about Stalin. It was not one of those pseudo-patriotic opuses in which brave children uncovered hidden spies; it was the beautiful, tender story of a girl emerging from adolescence. It was about love, friendship, happiness and suffering, a poem of life. An embittered man wrote it. He was a veteran of the Russian Civil War. He witnessed a lot of death, and the book proved his longing for life and his hope for a better future. That hope made him a volunteer when Germans attacked Russia in 1941. He was badly wounded in 1942. After recovery he lived as a recluse until he died in 1972. He never married. I think he was in love with his character Tanya, an idealistic, romantic youth of the upcoming generation. Although their happiness might have justified all those immense sacrifices he had made, in the end they would all perish. He never recovered his optimism.

In America, JD Salinger never recovered either. *The Catcher In the Rye* was published during the McCarthyism. I read it in the 1970s in Russia and it took me by surprise. His protagonist, Holden Caulfield was very much like myself—a thoughtful, vulnerable young man, lonely and hurt who was branded a loser by his peers. He lacked a trait so cherished in the American culture; the practice of taking every possible advantage of others. His supposed friends and acquaintances used him. Stradlater, his roommate at school, had him write an English essay for him. Maurice, a hotel elevator operator and a pimp, robbed and humiliated him. Phil Stable and others drew one of Holden's classmates, James Castle to suicide. These characters were the winners, and the loser

Holden didn't fit in. The book by JD Salinger has many layers and one is to examine the transformation of the boy in the process of becoming a man through self-awareness. In the end, Holden realizes his own worth, his potential and his power as an adult.

Russian poet and émigré Joseph Brodsky said in one of his poems,

"You suddenly realize yourself as a wholesome gift."

In Holden the nation had a good citizen, noble and self-confident. Having found himself, he finally fit in. It was the others who became the losers. I think that Holden was JD Salinger's response to McCarthyism that would victimize the good citizens. It would be impossible to victimize or humiliate Holden ever again. JD Salinger, the WWII veteran, the man who had smelled the burning flesh of war, as had Rouvim Fraerman, put his love and hate into his characters. Both Holden and Tanya came alive and proved their worthiness in the eternal fight for the humane.

Like Fraerman, JD Salinger lived a life of a recluse in Cornish, NH until he died in 2010. Both would be thrilled at the thought that Holden, an American might have had a spiritual connection with Tanya, a Russian. There were rye fields where Tanya lived, and people ate candies on the New Year. Holden would have loved it; even the hat he wore would be fitting in Russia. Good books about teenagers are full of what we, the Russians call 'noble sadness.' That's when both the author and a reader love the characters no matter what, and it is very rare, As rare as the spark in the total darkness. Nobody knows why the Russian book was called *The Wild Dog Dingo*. Nobody knows what Holden was to catch in the rye either. He only wanted the children not to fall into the ravine.

The issue of a character with self-awareness is the primary issue of all times. It is really a God's moment when you can read about such character and associate yourself with Tanya Sabaneeva, the teenage girl from the Russian Far East and Holden Caulfield, the boy in a red hat in New York. They both convey the message of invincible humanity. We must hear it.

Chapter 9

Memory Cherished

The leaves of memory seemed to make a mournful rushing in the dark...

H.W. Longfellow

КАПЛИ ДАТСКОГО КОРОЛЯ

Интересно, получится ли у меня это сделать...

С. Моэм

I wonder if I could make it seen...

S. Maugham

> Не знаю уж, получится едва ли,
> Я вспоминаю детства темный зал,
> В кинотеатре на окраине Москвы,
> Сидели мы, а может быть и вы.

Ах, Женя, Женечка, старинное кино,
Не верится, что было так давно,
Те капельки, что булькали, звеня,
И молодость садилась на коня,

Такие молодые, что хоть плачь,
И нет ни лагерей ни передач,
И голос Окуджавы в первый раз
Сквозь пушек гром доносится до нас.

Такое не срифмуешь наперед,
Как песенка та за душу берет.
Без меры кавалеры напились,
А капельки все без конца лились.

И в капельках как будто растворен,
Пропал войны последний батальон.
И снизошел на нас само собой
От короля, от датского покой.

Шептались потихоньку малыши,
И мой отец смеялся от души,
И старого экрана синева
Над солнечной дорогой пролегла.

Так через бремя памяти моей,
Звон капель давний слышен все сильней.
И если попадался мне фиал,
Его всегда до дна я выпивал.

The Danish King's Drops

Let's see if I can dream it once again,
A cinema with Dad and with my friends
Where we were lost and there we would remain
In never-never land that never ends.

Eugene Eugenochka and Katusha
A movie long ago and in our ears
The Danish King, its drops and we're in awe
As youth on horseback drives away our fears

So young they were, they made you want to cry
No labor camps just thrills and spills and more,
And Okudzava's voice will never die.
We hear it through a cannonade of war.

Not in advance it's rhymed. It's here and now.
That song, it reaches out to touch your soul,
And through the wine, they take a solemn vow
To keep the faith and let the good times roll

As drops dilute the last of battles fought,
Serenity replaces fear and strife.
The Danish drops have brought the peace we sought
And offered us an altered view of life.

My friends they whisper quite excitedly,
For life has taken on a golden glow,
And Dad laughs heartily to see their glee.
That he feels free is also good to know.

Fluidic memories of Danish King,
Eliminate the need to wear a frown.
I see now clearly what this life can bring.
Come fill the cup with drops. I'll drink them down.

The poem is about an episode when I watched an old war movie as a boy with my Dad and two friends. The movie was called 'Eugenie, Euginochka and Katyusha." It had nothing to do with the prescription drugs. Elixir of youth, maybe? How do you call a remedy for all evils, a drink of eternal peace, or perhaps a love potion? Native Americans knew about such a remedy, but alas, only their shadows remain as we show them on TV: mighty warriors on their transparent horses, only shadows now. No longer will they share their knowledge with us.

In my former country there was such a remedy. It was a song 'The Danish King Drops' that eased the pain. It was written by a poet, Bulat Okudzhava, whose father was arrested, tortured and executed, and whose mother was sentenced to ten years in prison when he was about eight years old. How can a person become a poet after that, I wonder? Okudzhava was a people's singer, he sang on the streets, at parties, in the halls and even in monasteries. He was a Dean of the bards, that strange tribe of people who wandered through the dimly lit jungle of our existence shining like small diamonds in the gutter. Their songs were those tiny drops of happiness and hope, which made us stronger and more resilient. They made it possible for us to live no matter what. It was especially important for the young people. While here in America, every young person, at times, copes with some kind of depression, some feeling of unworthiness, guilt or terrible loneliness, in Russia, that feeling was hereditary. It was as natural as those dimly lit streets, greasy kitchens and hopeless eyes of our parents. Instead of individual depressions we had the collective one that absorbed the whole nation.

There were no drugs or shrinks or anything. We had only the Danish King drops. We drank them in gulps and sipped to the end until the depression was no more.

Image By
Galiks
ID:589197608

Chapter 10

The Shadow

Midway in our lives' journey
I went astray from the shortest road
And woke to find myself
Alone in a dark wood....

Dante Alighieri
The Divine Comedy

Картины давнего детства,
Зачитанные тома,
Где слов немое соседство
Меня сводило с ума.

Словечко, решившее многое
Навеки в мозгу сидит,
Немецкое, колченогое,
Змеиное,"Плебисцит."

В далеком, французском Сааре
Дотоле неведомом мне,
За Рейх проголосовали,
К немецкой клонясь волне.

На миг всего мне почудилось,
Что будто я там рожден,
Гремит немецкая музыка
Под лотарингским дождем.

Фрацузской речи не слышно,
Соседи "Хорст Вессель" поют,
И факельный свет колышется,
Как огненный каракурт.

Страшнее нет осознания,
Что, заблудясь в карнавале,
По собственному желанию
Мы разум свой потеряли.

И поздно кричать, доказывать,
Друг-друга разубеждать.
А надо билеты заказывать
Пока еще можно бежать.

Поэтому вечерами
По старой своей примете,
Я в оперу собираюсь,
Поглядывать на соседей.

Затих шумок в бельетаже,
Погас театральный свет,
Заполнил клеточку каждый:
Быть с Гитлером, или нет.

THE SHADOW

Although a child, the *volumes* that I read
With silent words that spoke as with a scream
And thus reverberating in my head,
Relentlessly repeats a constant theme.

Forever in my mind it will abide,
One word of all the others I might cite,
A plebiscite or German volksentscheid,
A blazing day that ushered in the night.

A plebiscite in faraway French Saar,
With French and Germans both most unalike,
And Germans in their numbers did by far
Proclaim allegiance to the German Reich.

So real it seems, I sense that I was there.
Their German music pulsates in my ear.
With eyes aglaze, the blindness in their stare
Makes rationale and reason disappear.

No French is heard. "Horst Vessel" is the cry.
It's sung in shouts until their throats are raw.
Bereft of thoughts that anyone should die,
The fiery torches form the Swastika.

How horrible it is to contemplate
The loss of freedom with the loss of voice.
To realize the truth, but all too late,
Rabidly to lose one's way by choice.

Too late, too late for argument and blame.
What hope there is awaits another day.
There's nothing now to wash away the shame.
There's nothing now but just to run away.

There should be other avenues, although
Escape it seems is all one has, sans hope,
So nightly to the opera I go,
Observing how my neighbors choose to cope.
Lights dim, noise stops a sudden solitude.
It's now in darkness answers must be sought,
A crucial search for moral rectitude:
Is it to be with Hitler's horde, or not?

This is a warning. It is customary to think that political disasters, dictatorships, police states, or genocide happen due to some sudden scheming intrigue, a coup perhaps. Those things do take place, of course, but very frequently evil creeps in slowly, gradually, when freedom is surrendered step by step by the people themselves. Usually it happens during tough times when there are economic hardships, political corruption or when the majority is just afraid of the unknown. Three years before the WWII, the Saar district between Germany and France was given a choice in a referendum to stay with France or reunify with Hitler's Germany. Of course, many people there were of German origin and they were not happy that after WWI those territories were allocated to France. It is highly probable that they were peaceful people and Hitler with his marching storm-troopers did not appeal to them either. But when the time to choose came, they voted for him. It was a free vote by modern standards. They voted for Hitler because he spoke their language, because it seemed simple enough to reunify, and because he promised to liberate them. True Germans, though from mixed races like Jewish, French and others, voted simply for something familiar: for German faces on the streets, for beer instead of wine, for Berlin taxes instead of Paris ones, for sausages instead of pate. They voted for a way of life they were used to. He promised them safety and superiority and they sold their souls.

They sold their souls but there is no happiness in superiority. Freedom and happiness can be achieved only on equal grounds, only together. If you take possession of the people and make them miserable, you can never be happy because of the fear that they might overturn the things sooner or later.

Image By
Natali Li
ID:475127758

Chapter 11

Song of Love

A coward is incapable of exhibiting love; it is a prerogative of the brave

M. Gandhi

ПЕСНЯ ЛЮБВИ

В королевском замке тишина,
Влажным мраком тянет от реки,
За ворота в ночь ушла жена,
И король страдает от тоски.

Сколько было их-не сосчитать
Среди поражений и побед,
Приглашал художников писать
Каждое лицо запечатлеть.

Что-то было с ними и прошло,
Следа не оставило в душе,
Чуть до эшафота не дошло
Пару раз, но обошлось без жертв,

Лишь ее увидел и узнал-
Канули они все в пустоту
Чуть с коня на землю не упал,
Встретив неземную красоту.

Счастье не на троне, а в семье
В тихих разговорах за столом
И в бессонной ночи при Луне,
Не от заговоров и послов.

Между башнями растаял лед
Вишни под балконом зацвели,
Ранняя весна, солнцеворот,
Музыканты, скрипки, соловьи.

И страна в те годы расцвела
Без походов, войн и без костров.
Непогода стороной прошла,
И никто не потрясал основ.

Дети подросли, семья жила.
В солнечный и безмятежный день.
Труппа театральная пришла
И дала спектакль во дворе.

Факелы горели по углам,
Молодой премьер читал пролог,
Королеву в ложе увидал,
Положил к ногам ее цветок.

И когда последний из возов
За ворота замка вышел прочь
Королева словно от оков
Отряхнулась и пропала в ночь.

Он погоню следом не послал
И в набат звонить не разрешил.
Лишь коня поутру оседлал
И вдогон отправился один.

Без дороги по полям седым,
Целый день скакал, не отдохнув,
Спешился в воротах городских,
Бедным пешеходом проскользнул.

У старинной ратуши простой
Шел большой спектакль на мостовой,
И народный танец заводной
Танцевал актер с его женой.

Музыка гремела, дым стоял,
Как горели у нее глаза!
Тихо в стороне ои постоял,
И уехал, как прошла гроза.

Через год у крепостных ворот,
Где сошлись висячие мосты
Засветился горделивый свод
Необыкновенной красоты.

Каждый вечер поворотный круг
Чудеса для зрителей являл
И король, как старый, добрый друг
Вальсы с примадонной танцевал,

Может так оно и быть должно,
Без кошмаров, крови и плетей
Лишь любви открытое окно
Справедливость-сила королей.

Ведь любовь тому и воздает,
Кто сумел себя преодолеть.
И веселый ангелов полет
Среди тьмы бесстрашно рассмотреть.

Song of Love

Both King and castle were in silence now,
A humid mist arising with the breeze
The Queen had left her king with heavy brow
To say the least, the King was not at ease

Oh, many were the faces he'd recall
From long ago, defeats and victories.
He even had them painted, one and all
To keep them fresh within his memories

With soul untouched no matter what occurred,
And though the scaffolding was twice in place
There were no executions, both deferred
Eternally, on order of his Grace.

So, when the king first saw and recognized
A lass with beauty never seen before.
And slipping from his horse, was paralyzed,
His sought for Queen she'd be for evermore.

The throne provides no happiness, just rights.
It's at a quiet table love will peak
Or underneath the moon on sleepless nights.
Discussions yes, but not of matters bleak.

Old winter thawed, the frost and ice gave way
To cherry blossoms over hill and dale.
The sun of spring had chased the cold away
With sounds of violin and nightingale.

It was as though the country came to life.
There were no wars or battles to be won.
With no more grief or sadness, no more strife
And none to wish the status quo undone.

With families the best of times held sway,
That was until one sunny day that spring.
A company of actors came their way,
Performing for his lady and the King.

The prologue was delivered by their lead,
Who, gazing at the Queen with bold conceit,
In hopes that she might wither and accede
He dared to place a flower at her feet.

On leaving, as his wagon passed the gates,
The queen, with head awhirl, forsook her plight.
She recklessly submitted to her fates,
And with her love, they vanished into night.

The King decided not to have her traced,
Nor even let this tragedy be known.
His majesty, not wanting her debased,
Determined that he'd find her on his own.

Across the fields he galloped without rest.
Until he came upon the nearest town.
The green-eyed monster having been repressed,
On foot he entered but without his crown.

The people filled the square to see the show,
A reenactment of the former scene.
The King, aware his love he must forgo,
Observed the actor dancing with his queen

He saw her bliss. Her eyes were all aglow.
Because he wore his heart upon his sleeve
He couldn't hide the hurt. He had to know.
So bowing quietly he took his leave.

Before the Castle gates in just one year,
A beautiful new theatre was built.
The company returned for a premiere
The Queen appeared without a hint of guilt.

The stage, a place where miracles took place,
When every night the people would convene,
And afterwards the King with charm and grace,
Would dance the prima donna as his Queen.

And like the king might we be selfless too?
Eliminate all thoughts of bloody war,
With love, a window, starting life anew,
A king with justice, hear the lion roar.

For love rewards the brave, the bold, the Knight
Who overcomes himself to make a mark,
Who fearlessly enjoys the Angels' flight
Although, at times the outlook can be dark.

Poetry cannot exist without love. Vladimir Vysotsky wrote, "Souls of the lovers are destined to forever walk in flowers." And here is Emily Dickinson, a hundred years before him, "If I can stop one heart from breaking, I shall not live in vain." Choose love for yourself, find a connection.

Along with my professional career here in America, for some time I taught Russian language and introduction to Russian culture to a group of young professionals. How can you introduce a culture? Where do you start? After some consideration I started with the female names. The most popular first names in Russia are Вера, Надежда, Любовь. (Faith, Hope, and Love). Faith and Hope are fairly common names in the USA too. The third one is usually used as a middle or second name.

I daresay this pattern reflects the attitude towards love in the whole of Western Civilization to a certain extent. That is the word 'love' is abused in many ways. Turn on the TV and the first thing you hear is Love. Love of food, love of exercise, "love your country," making love, love of your car, love of God, love of success, Love, Love, Love.

I think it is much misused. You really cannot 'love' something which is not alive, like cheese, car or country. I guess, you can like those things or even admire them. General Robert Lee, in expressing his genuine love for Virginia was most likely expressing his highest feeling of duty, an obligation to the land of his ancestors. But, I doubt that he loved it as one would love things that are alive. You love a man, a woman, a dog, even a tree. Something that grows, evolves, changes. Something which needs you. Love is Help.

As any real Help, it has one strict condition and that is that it has to be accepted freely, on an equal basis. There are no superiors in Love. Even when you love a dog you become one for a while.

Love is mysterious, enchanting and difficult, but not cruel. In the general scheme of things Love always brings happiness to everybody, It is just a matter of understanding.

Image By
Aradaphotography
ID:260998763

Chapter 12

Murder of the Poet

Poet murdered...

G. Apollinaire

Проездом на Поезде Через Елабугу

Отказываюсь быть

В бедламе нелюдей...
М. Цветаева

I refuse to live in the non-human bedlam

M. Tsvetaeva

Как тяжело посметь
Коснуться этих тем,
Проснуться и прозреть,
Когда был слеп и нем.

Как страшно начинать
Об этом разговор,
Уж лучше оборвать,
И выйти в коридор.

Чтоб не видал никто
То мертвое лицо,
Промокшее пальто,
Последнее кольцо.

Никто не удержал,
Никто не уберег,
Никто не помешал
И не предостерег.

На Западе чума
В кладбищенской тиши,
И на Востоке тьма,
Ни проблеска в глуши.

От дьявольских затей
Пропала ни за грош
Наперсница царей,
Наследница вельмож.

От мужества души,
От щедрости добра,
Ты мишурою лжи
Прельститься не могла.

Веревка с потолка
Протянута змеей,
Как черная рука
Проклятье над страной!

И хуже всех смертей
Пожизненно звучит:
В бед-ла-ме не-лю-дей
От-ка-зы-ва-юсь жить.

In the Train Passing Through Elabuga, Russia

How difficult to dare and touch
Those all forbidden themes and find
That once awake and inasmuch
You must have been both dumb and blind

No reason to exchange our views,
There's nothing much we might achieve.
Such horrors we cannot excuse.
T'is better that we stop and leave.

It's probable no one will see
The ghastly face as there you hung.
Your wedding ring. You may be free,
But what you gave will go unsung.

So, no one stopped and no one cared
And no one rose to interfere.
And no one cautioned, no one dared.
So bleak the atmosphere, austere.

As though a plague had struck the West
The silence of the grave held fast
And in the East one might have guessed,
A pall of darkness, deep and vast.

You spoke with czars, you spoke with kings
Your ancestry most noble was,
And true to life, the poet sings.
A life expired without a cause.

So strong your soul, a soul unmatched
Your kindness was so evident
That from the lies you stood detached
The truth became your testament.

Your hanging rope, much like a snake
Coiled round and round, perverse and worse,
Made any cause or sense opaque.
Black handed evil was the curse.

It's not enough with all the dead,
To live with all the muck and ruck
To stay and to endure instead
A life with bedlam run amok.

Anna Akhmatova, the great Russian poet commented once on an error in the biographical book on her which was written by an American writer, "He wrote that I was in Paris in 1936 but it wasn't me. It was Marina Tsvetaeva. I can understand, though; someone told him that there was a Russian woman-poet in Paris at that time and he decided it was me. To imagine two women-poets living at the same time would be too tough for him." In 1941 Marina Tsvetaeva, also the great Russian poet, a genius of the first order, hanged herself in Elabuga, Russia when she found out that her son was to be conscripted for war. By that time her husband had been already executed and her daughter was arrested and sentenced to a concentration camp. She was a pure soul, integrity personified, the best of the best. I am very bitter in this poem. Something is terribly wrong.

Chapter 13

The Prophet

It is a man that makes the truth great, not the truth that makes a man great

Confucius

А. Галичу
(песня)

Кто-то должен, презрев усталость,
Наших мертвых стеречь покой...
А. Галич

Someone should stay behind and guard the peace of our dead..
A. Galich

"А художник-это и есть несчастный случай....."
Из фильма

An artist-is an unhappy accident
From the movie

Да простится ему,
Что сказал наудачу, в запале,
Что позднее в далеком Париже старался забыть.
Мертвецам ни к чему
Покаянный трезвон на гитаре,
И дорогу кровавую смерти нельзя полюбить.

Сведено все на нет,
По живому последнюю нитку
Перерезать навеки с кладбища к живым выходя,
Хоть оглох и ослеп,
Но нащупал рукою калитку,
И в последнем усилии, с плачем ушел как дитя.

Разберутся, поймут,
По широкой дороге свободы
Шли не ангелы, люди,
Греховный покинувши дом,

И на праведный суд,
Он надежду пронес через годы,
С той монеткой, которой
Платил за последний паром.

Он несчастного случая сгинул...
Последнее верно,
Поплывут облака в Магадан,
Проливаясь дождем.

Грохнул ящик стола,
Тихий вздох пролетел по Вселенной,
Никому не задуть огонька,
Что мы в церкви зажжем.

Мы помянем его,
За нелегкую, вольную душу,
За надрыв, за болезнь,
За последний проигранный бой.

И под звездным огнем,
Сам Господь нам предложит послушать,
Предрассветную песнь,
Что бессменный поет часовой.

To Alexander Galich
(song)

For what he did in anger, we forgive.
In gay Paree at last, he could forget.
The dead need no atonement for they live,
Although the road to death remains a threat.

Amazing how it all will come to naught
When living threads are severed for all time.
You leave the grave, it isn't what you sought.
You cry because your poem cannot rhyme

You hope that people might just sort it out,
Not angels but in truth, we human kind,
That freedom is the path, there is no doubt,
The only guarantee of peace of mind

Such was the hope he carried and with pride
Along with justice for the tried and true,
And with a coin for Charon's ferry ride
He sought at last, the peace that was his due.

An accident they say, it may be true,
But should the sands of time prove otherwise,
His voice with song, will stir our hearts anew.
His words as rain will pour from cloudy skies.

Across the universe a sigh was heard.
His cogent voice was stilled but not his plea.
The Church ignites, his plea goes undeterred
For who would violate a church decree?

We'll say our prayers for him and for his soul
Unhappy though he was but free at last
His battle lost. He failed to reach his goal
But did he fail? His hoped for die's been cast.

As God on high takes up his fervent cry
A cry in song for justice by the bard,
A bard appointed by a God on high,
The Sentinel forever standing guard.

This poem is dedicated to a man whom I admired and loved, although I never knew him. He was a poet and a singer, a fighter and an exile.

He perished in fire in Paris after being expelled from the country he adored. One of his most beautiful poems is called "When I Return." Now I understand why he wrote it. That's after I met with the

IMMORTALS OF LENINGRAD

I stood in the Franz Snyders Hall in the Le Hermitage museum in Leningrad (currently St. Petersburg) when I heard that voice,

"This is the only place you can see that fish. We eradicated the species through 300 years."

The voice belonged to a shabby, middle-aged man dressed in a worn vested suite over the sweater and winter boots. A branch with green leaves stuck out of his pocket.

"A starving scientist like you," continued the stranger "could theorize that this indigenous Russian fish found its way to the Dutch fishery, where Snyderz spotted it. Some Russian aristocrat bought the painting with his beloved fish and brought it back for us to see now what we had lost."

"How do you know I am a scientist?" I asked.

"So I am right about hunger? You have been visiting this hall of food for the third time. Also, you are curious beyond fear. Everyone else left when I started talking. I detect a faint smell of alcohol. Compulsive drunkards do not frequent this place though. Thus you could be a scientist or a medical student. Medical students prefer nudity. Ergo, you are a scientist. Let's continue our discussions in Saigon."

Saigon was the street name for the only cafe in the city with decent coffee and unlimited time to stay. We proceeded to the smoky corner, where I was introduced to the Immortals. Long ago such people were called the vagants, the free scholarly spirits. They were artists, painters, actors, dancers, who spent their days working in obscure theaters, restoring old churches or teaching children in small studios. Some were aspiring writers or activists like my self-appointed mentor who called himself the St. Petersburg Ghost of Greenpeace.

"I plant trees," he explained to me. "They call me crazy but I don't care. We do what we consider right. That's why we seldom have scientists here. They are too self-confident, too deterministic, and therefore-mediocre. Look how they are running away from religion. Whereas science and religion are connected through love. Ivan Pavlov knew that when he converted back to Christianity. You seem open-minded. But for you to become an apprentice we need something more tangible. Do you have anything to offer?"

I offered my daily supply of free milk coming from the chemistry research lab. They needed it. Leningrad took its toll on the needy. Most of them avoided the mandatory city police dwelling registration by renting rooms in communal apartments or in the slums. None of them had steady income and they never complained about anything. They spent their time talking and learning, sharing views and theories, continuously challenging their minds like databases in a vivid environment of imagination. In the Northern Palmyra this is accomplished through walking around.

Our tours were the never-ending discoveries. We would pay a visit to the Gorokhovaya, the first headquarters of the Soviet Secret Police. From that place the river of blood and tears made its way to the back entrance of Smolny where Kirov was murdered and proceeded waywardly throughout the country, peppering the territory with Big Houses, the gates of Hell. The milestone for the city historical gates and basements would be the gates of Mikhailovsky Castle where Paul, the First was killed and Dostoevsky studied engineering. The small gate on the Katherine's Channel would mark the place where Sofia Perovskaya signaled to blow up the Tsar Alexander II. From there it was not far to an abandoned basement, the former Stray Dog poets' cabaret, frequented by Anna Akhmatova when she was young and in love.

To sing we would gather at the place of our music guru, the corpulent dame with a voice thick from heavy smoking. Zongs would be correct definition, with their origin in German urban ballads, enriched by Russian sense of profound sadness. The guru lady accompanied the guitars on the piano and improvised, asking us for the topics. I was complimented for finding a poem good enough to become a zong. There were also movies and theater. One night it would be a barely lit culture house hall with an amateur company staging a Ionesco drama. On another night we would go to a study auditorium, with showing of "The Mirror" by Tarkovsky or "Amarcord" by Fellini.

We argued passionately. Controversy was as natural as an iceberg stuck under the Palace Bridge in May. We discussed science, arts, religion, nature, history, social issues, but never politics or money. In the dim light of Saigon or in the icy room with window looking at the brick wall we dissected Chayanov's agricultural society theories and Stanislavsky's acting system. It was teamwork in its finest, cemented by the perception that mere facts mean nothing without the touch of heart. That subjectivity, that individual bias developed the human wisdom. We relived the events of the centuries: talked with Van Gogh, danced with Isadora Duncan, drank with Byron and Edgar Poe. It takes time to fall in love with the process. And when it happens, the apprenticeship is over.

My research assignment came to an end. One night I rose quietly in the middle of a heated debate and left for the railway station. There I boarded a carriage and sat in the dark until the train started to move. I looked out at the platform and saw them standing with guitars in their hands, singing the farewell song under the silver streams. That very song I heard ten years later, on that dreadful night when I was leaving the country for good, "Again I am leaving you, my love and my destiny. I am smiling at you, please, don't cry..."

In the US I watched the series about Immortal Highlander and imagined the Gathering. No beheadings, no blood, no struggle for power, just wisdom shared and songs beside the fire. Forever, forever.

Chapter 14

I Loved My Friend

I loved my friend.
He went away from me.
There's nothing more to say.
I loved my friend..

W. Shakespeare

О Викторе Некрасове

"В окопах Сталинграда "-не читал
Хоть шепот в детстве помню очень явно,
Учителям вопросы задавал,
Но правды не услышал и подавно.

Еще я помню, было мне шесть лет,
Неясная тревога ощущалась,
Игрушечный мой щелкал пистолет,

Некрасов, Куреневка, все смешалось...
Потом Крещатик помню в ранний час,
Нас ожидает Кинопанорама,
Торопимся на утренний сеанс
"Смотри, Некрасов,"-говорит мне мама.

Двенадцать лет молчали провода,
И это имя прозвучало снова.
Уехал за границу навсегда...
Умолкло недосказанное слово.

Потом еще прошло пятнадцать лет,
И следом я отправился в изгнанье.
Хотелось познакомиться, сосед.
Но опоздал, напрасное старанье.

Его последние печальные слова
И все о нем читаю вне России.
Еще одна скатилась голова,
В борьбе со злом внезапно обессилев.

Его не видел, с ним не говорил,
И за батоном для него не сбегал.
Но кажется , что брата пережил,
Так хоть могилу надо бы проведать.

Скромна, наверное, ему под стать
Солдату правды лишнего не надо.
Куда как трудно сорок лет стоять,
Начав еще с окопов Сталинграда.

Но иногда мне чудится карниз,
Которым Бабий Яр был огорожен.
Стоит Некрасов, смотрит, смотрит вниз,
А головы поднять уже не может.

On Victor Nekrasov

Though I heard a lot of whispering at school.
About Nekrasov's book of Stalingrad.
No mention by the teachers was the rule.
No answers to the questions that I had.

When I was six, my mind had gone bizarre.
Perhaps my toy, a gun, no longer fun.
Nekrasov, Kurenevka, Baby Yar,
It seemed that suddenly they all were one.

Then to the early movie, Mom and me,
Had gone together on Khreshatik street.
And suddenly she called out "Look Son, see.
"The great Nekrasov. One day you must meet."

But twelve years passed, and then I understood.
His message that I didn't get before.
Alas, by then he'd gone abroad for good
To find some solace on a foreign shore.

Then I in exile too, had hoped to see
My neighbor hoping I might share his cost,
However, such a joy was not to be,
For I was late. The dream and he were lost.

But now, away from Russia, I can read
About his life, his last sad words and more,
The words humanity had better heed.
Lest we succumb to evil we abhor.

I never met or talked with him, I fear.
So much as bread, to him, I never gave.
Yet in his memory we persevere.
I should at least pay homage at his grave.

To face existence when there's naught but strife.
Aside from truth, 'twas little to be had.
To stand and be defiant all your life
Beginning in a trench at Stalingrad.

I see him standing now at Baby Yar.
His head is bowed in anguish and despair.
His stony figure frozen. It's bizarre.
Becoming one of them, the victims there.

There's nothing more to say. Except maybe that not all of your friends you know personally. If Victor Nekrasov lived in the age of Facebook, we would communicate, but I do remember the tomb of Machiavelli in the Santa Croce Cathedral in Florence, where it says 'No words'. No words.

Chapter 15

In Memoriam

Погоны Андерса–как пачки танцовщины..

Н. Гербаневская

The Anders' army shoulder-straps resemble a ballet-dancer's outfit..

N. Gerbanevskaya

Полякам из Армии Андерса, павшим под Монте-Кассино

(To Polish soldiers from the Anders' army, who died at Monte-Cassino, Italy, 1944)

Как давно это было, а может быть только вчера,
Посполито рушенье спасало Европу от турок.
Я смотрю на картину у храма Святого Петра.
Вместо шлемов и лат вижу зелень военных тужурок.

Палаши и значки офицеров, винтовки солдат,
От сибирских морозов глаза их еще голубее.
Это движется Польша, грохочет варшавский набат,
И штандарт Вестерплятте над ними бестрепетно реет.

В итальянском раю смерть глядит через щелку с высот,
Из развалин аббатства несет человеческим мясом,
Пулеметом прострелян единственный горный проход,
И врага не достать, хоть снарядов и дали с запасом.
По сигналу вы все поднялись как огонь голубой,
Будто Грюнвальда клич вас позвал на последнюю битву.
О жолнеры, для многих из вас это был первый бой.
У подножия горы сотворили монахи молитву.

Я смотрю на картину у храма Святого Петра,
Как прекрасны хоругви в зените бессмертья и славы.
Но от горя и страха седеет моя голова,
Вас в кавярнях своих никогда не увидит Варшава.

Перед входом в Сикстинскую залу я вам поклонюсь,
Молодым и прекрасным в своем благородном порыве,
Я прощенья прошу, я за всех перед вами винюсь.
Уберечь не смогли вас, простите, мои дорогие!

Бесконечное жаркое Солнце, да будет оно
Вашим счастьем и вашим последним, решительным чудом.
Вы воскреснете все, на пиру молодое вино
Потечет по бокалам под грохот победных салютов.

О, старинная Польша, прими своих верных сынов,
Освяти их крылами , поднявшись из пепла и тлена,
Пусть гремит Полонез, заглушая паденье оков,
И ликует с народом ожившее сердце Шопена.

LOOKING AT THE PAINTING AT VATICAN

(To Polish soldiers from the Anders' army, who died at Monte-Cassino, Italy, 1944)

It was so long ago, or was it only yesterday,
when gallant Polish forces stopped the Turkish charge,
and saved a grateful European continent?

I see it there, the ancient painting captures all,
but suddenly, Monte-Cassino Can it be,
again the blue-eyed Poles but now in uniforms of green?

The bells of Warsaw toll as Poland moves once more,
andoverhead the flag of Westerplatte returns,
for war is war and history repeats itself.

The enemy! They have you zeroed in.
Machinegun fire! It rakes your only path.
The enemy! They seem invincible,
While up above, the Abbey smells of burning flesh.

Although for some, it is your first exchange,
The haunting call of Grunvald spurs you on.
The roaring din of battle from above,
The silence of the monks at prayer below.
I look again, and there on high the banners fly.
Immortal fame and glory rests on every head,
But then, my head grows dark with pain to realize;
the coffee shops of Warsaw are no longer theirs.

I bow to youth, sublime and noble in their feat,
And with the bow, I beg forgiveness for us all,
the older ones that stay protected and alive.
The ones who in our fear would send you off to die.

Allow the endless sun to mark your miracle,
and grant eternal happiness, so well deserved.
And with your resurrection, may you drink young wine
While all the sky will fill with victory salutes.

Oh, ancient Poland meet and great your loyal sons.
to watch them rise like Phoenix, cleanly from the ash.
Let's hear the Polonaise above the falling chains
Proclaiming Chopin's heart to be once more alive,
and let once more a grateful people celebrate.

I am a Russian Jew. From my father's side we are Polish Jews and from my mother's side we are Ukrainian Jews. That reflects my generational experience. My grandfather's family lived in Poland for a while, but Poland was not good for them. They had to run away from pogroms in 1919 and they went to the East. There is, though, a special feature found in all Jews as the Russian philosopher Bulgakov stated. They absorb the cultures of the nations in which they reside. Our family absorbed Polish romanticism. We had books on Poland's great battles like Grunewald. That's why when we visited Vatican in Y2001 we didn't miss that painting, right in front of the entrance to the Sistine Chapel. It depicted the triumphant entry of the Polish forces into Vienna after they saved it from Turks in the 18th Century. I couldn't help but remember the story of Monte-Cassino in WWII. Italians told me the story long before, during my first stay in Italy in 1989 as a UN refugee. It's amazing how much you can learn and understand while just sitting at the street corner under the piercing sun, in a strange land, surrounded by local people you really like, but whose language you do not know. I verified it afterwards with the Italian historian who knew English.

The 13th Century mountain Abbey of Monte-Cassino was considered sacrosanct among the locals. When the Allies approached in 1944 many people, especially the poor ones left their homes and went to the Abbey for shelter. They felt safe there being protected by God's own walls. Germans knew about this and left the Abbey unfortified while leaving the Allies with the wrong impression that it was. Eager for an easy victory, and thinking it was occupied by the Germans, the Allies mercilessly bombed the monastery, killing thousands of civilians. After the bombing was over Germans returned and quickly and skillfully fortified the ruins. The Allies advanced in the morning to take over the strategic position and were promptly and painfully repelled. Again and again the Allies tried in vain to take the ruins of the Abbey. Finally, they sent in the Polish Anders' Army, consisting of volunteers, all of Polish origin. The Poles took the challenge and, like the first all-black regiment in the American Civil War at Fort Wagner, they charged and died, but the monastery was taken. This is the story of Monte-Cassino in 1944. The Anders Army was commissioned and armed in Russia. Those young soldiers dreamed of liberating Warsaw and of celebrating in its streets. In the poem, I tried my best to express what I felt as I stood gazing at that painting. Nobody noticed me crying for my dear Poland. People hurried by on their way to the Sistine Chapel, having forgotten Monte-Cassino. How can you blame them? It happened so long ago.

Image BY
iQoncept
ID:83141602

Chapter 16

The Lynchpin Chapter

You will not find poetry anywhere unless you bring some of it with you..

Joseph Joubert

Рождественский Перерыв

У каждого поэта есть провинция...
С. ГУДЗЕНКО

Every Person has a Province
S. Gudzenko

Провинция справляет рождество..

И. БРОДСКИЙ
The Province Celebrates Christmas..
J.Brodsky

Не пишется, не дышится, скорее

Прочь от стола, подальше от металла,
Быть может новая пора настала,
И можно запросто поговорить.

Когда-то ведь трагический кузнечик
Мечтал о разговоре в подворотне,
На лестнице, у корабельной сходни,
Все порывался дьяволу звонить.

А это было вовсе и не нужно.
Нечистый за ближайшим поворотом,
С готовностью бормочет заклинанья,
Инструкции как души уловить.

Ему читай, он не устанет слушать.
Одну строку прокручивай по-новой,
Неправда, что божественные строфы,
Нас вдохновляют ангелы сложить,

Скорее чертенята... Пляшут духи,
Над ужасами, глупостью и кровью,
Что первыми приходят к изголовью,
В тех снах, где начинаются стихи,

Приправленные яростным усильем,
Проснуться оглядеться, раскопаться,
До твердой почвы наконец добраться,
Увидеть свет-и голову сложить.

Какая разница, какого цвета,
Случайный демон был, что нашептал
В беспамятном полуночном кошмаре,
Тот сладкий полубред о черной шали,
Что сквозь столетья можно пропустить.

Вначале было слово....Что ж, наверное,
Был шепот под чужими небесами,
То свет, то тень, царило ожиданье,
Покуда крик не возвратится эхом,
В котором отразилось божество.

Как новая земля дана свобода,
Поэзии одной лишь в обладанье,
Хорошая в провинции погода,
Коль повезет, так справим Рождество!

A POET'S CHRISTMAS BREAK

Can't write, can hardly catch my breath,
I weep, a captive of my pen and desk.
It's time the poet's speak or else it's death.
A life in silent exile is grotesque
The Grasshopper in exile knew it well.

His one and only dream was to be heard.
Assuming that it meant a plea to hell,
He called upon the Devil undeterred.

But lo, round every corner demons wait
To catch the souls and stir the poets muse,
And even if their presence speaks of hate,
Its fodder for the mill that poets use.

It is not true that verses most divine
Are only for the angels to devise,
Nor is it left for them to mark the line
That falls between the evil and the wise.

So devilish demons aid the poet's cause.
They dance around and over blood and mire
And into sordid dreams that give us pause
To realize a truth that's born of fire.

It's from these dreams the poet adds his bit.
He's forced to come awake and look around
To see the light. Though he may die for it,
He struggles till he reaches solid ground.

Who cares from whence the wisest verses leap.
It's better that we know the truth they bring,
And just as with the Persian shawl they seep
Through centuries as through the wedding ring.

Poetic freedom under hostile skies,
A freedom only poets can define.
"I must be heard" the woeful poet cries,
And any blessed echo is divine.

So, if in time, we do not run amok,
But hear and heed poet's voice and pen,
The weather's fine, and with a little luck,
We'll celebrate our Christmas once again.

I quote from an unusual source:

"Good friends, my readers who peruse this book
Be not offended whil'st on it you look
Denude yourselves of all deprav'd affection
For it contains no badness, nor infection
T'is true that it brings forth to you no birth
Of any value but in point of mirth:

Thinking therefore how sorrow might you minde
Consume I could not apter subject finde;
One inch of joy surmounts a grief of pain
Because to laugh is proper to the man."

F. Rabelais
To the Readers of "Gargantua and Pantagruel," 1500s

The quote above is a lynchpin of a huge book, full of sidebars and digressions. It is complicated, multilayered and stitched together like a medieval sail. Whoever takes on a challenge of reading that book can easily become bored, angry and frustrated. The wise reader, however, should return to the statement above and reread it, for it follows you on a journey to understanding. The Christmas Break poem serves the same purpose; it follows the reader through a maze of Russian/English poetry and associated discussions. When I wrote this poem I did not have to think too much. It came to me that to fully appreciate both the book and the process you need sometimes to let it go, to look at it from aside, to clear your mind. I implore every reader whenever he/she feels bored or totally lost to return to this poem, suffer and celebrate with me.

Suffering is relative, though. Russian poet Ossip Mandelshtam (the Grashopper) suffered much more than me. He had no person to even read his verses to. I am lucky beyond imagination.

You have to love what you do. I am blessed with my engineering profession. I can build those beautiful, complex machines. But there is a connection between engineering, science and poetry. A poet builds his own ship, always ghostly, roaming about the sea like the Flying Dutchman always heading for the land, the mysterious, beautiful, bountiful land called Freedom.

WITCHCRAFT AT SALEM VILLAGE.

Chapter 17

My American Reference Point Salem, MA

She (Martha Corey) declared to two brethren that she did not think there were any witches...

Charles P. Upham
Salem Witchcraft
Volume 2, 1867

'One of the practical lessons inculcated by the history that has now been released is that no duty is more certain, none more important, than a free and fearless expression of opinion by all persons, on all occasions. No wise or philosophical person would think of complaining of the diversities of sentiment it is likely to develop. Such diversities are the vital principle of free communities and the only elements of popular intelligence. If the right to utter them is asserted by all and for all, tolerance is secured, and no inconvenience results. It is probable that there were many persons in 1692 who doubted the propriety of the proceedings at their commencement, but who were afterwards prevailed upon to fall into the current and swell the tide. If they had all discharged their duty to their country and their consciences by freely and boldly uttering their disapprobation and declaring their dissent, who can tell but the whole tragedy might have been prevented? and if it might, the blood of the innocent may be said, in one sense, to be upon their heads.'

Charles W. Upham
Salem Witchcraft, Volume 2, 1867.

Салем, Массачуссетс, 2007

Здесь вешали людей,
На тех деревьях, что так чудовищно
Искривлены, провиты как будто-бы веревкою,
На ветках серых, будто опаленных огнем веков,
Висели люди, в общем-то немного,
Всего-то девятнадцать, Мы потом
За триста с лишним лет немало наворочали и нечем
Нам тут гордиться, разве-что лишь тем, что в Салеме,
У старого кладбища я
Представил себе статую Бегущей,
И Фрези Грант так хорошо смотрелась
Простерши руки к морю. Здесь Александр Грин
Увиделся бы с Готорном; они-бы
друг-друга поняли. Но нет ее, сегодня
Я уезжаю-эти вот деревья, да голос Марты Кори:
-Нету ведьм!-я уношу с собой, хотя и не совсем
согласен с нею, но пусть уж будет по ее-все ж лучше
С умным потерять, чем с дураком найти.
Я оглянулся-и дерево кивнуло мне в знак братства.
Я вернусь.

SALEM, MASSACHUSETTS, 2007

They hanged the people here,
For witches, on those trees,
ghostly trees so ghoulishly gnarled.
charred in the inferno of infinity.
Oh, it was not that many. just nineteen.
In the years since,
we've made every effort to improve.

Little to be proud of.

And now, right here in Salem Massachusetts,
at the old cemetery,
I imagine the statue of Frezi Grant,
In Alexander Green's "Running on the Waves"
hands outstretched to sea, as to the future
How Green, in Russia and Hawthorne, here,
would have understood, one the other.
So far apart in space and time

There is no statue though.

And as I take my leave,
It's with those trees
And Martha Corey's voice.

"There are no witches."

"You are no big deal after all," I said to myself. I moved from one country to another, survived immigration and refugee settlements, secured employment, made a life for my family, helped my wife to study and succeed, worked with lots of people. Then I read about Martha Corey and how she stood up in 1692 and merely said, "There are no witches." I gasped when I read that because I remembered how many times I had agreed with foolish assertions, accepted ignorance and disregarded common sense; and how many people were hurt because of my cowardice and shallowness. An elderly woman more than three hundred years ago, with an open mind took a revolutionary step and calmly stated the truth, knowing all too well the danger she was facing. "Ignorance is a demonic force," said Karl Marx. One very educated and very smart Frenchman also said, "If someone accuses me of trying to destroy the Notre-Dame Cathedral I will run away as fast as possible." Senseless accusations tell us that we are targeted. Martha Corey knew. She said what she said anyway and paid for it with her life.

The six hundred accused people in Salem were all heroes, even the toddlers, and the nineteen of them that were hanged paid the price for all. None confessed to being a witch, though all, except for Martha Corey, admitted that witches did indeed exist. They were all good, decent, and sometimes outstanding people (like John Procter), but only Martha stood on her own conviction. Alone, in the dark she stood, and in that moment she joined the giants of Humanity from Copernicus to Stephan Lux. Copernicus could have risked less. He was neither accused of sorcery nor burned at stake. Maybe only Stephan Lux, that humble Hungarian photographer who killed himself on the floor of the League of Nations in 1936, carrying a briefcase full of anti-Nazi documents can be called a Hero on a saintly level like Martha.

Humility clears your vision. Salem, Massachusetts is my kind of town on the sea. That feeling grew even stronger when I strolled through the House Of The Seven Gables. It was a seafarer's house. Alexander Green would have loved to live in such a house with navigation maps on the walls and sextant on the captain's desk like he was on board of 'Running On Waves'. Right away I thought that he must have read Hawthorne's novels.

Alexander Green was a romantic, a rare fish in the Russian pond. When his stories were first published people thought they were translations. His real name was Alexander Grinevsky and he was born in Viatka, Russia, very far from the sea. His first story was called 'The Reno Island'. That island was in the country he invented, somewhere between Europe and America. I suspected that it was somewhere in Central America; where else could you imagine a galleon with purple sails from his love story 'The Purple Sails'?

People in Hawthorne's times may have been buried ashore, but they lived on and from the sea and died at sea. In Alexander Green's time, at the beginning of the 20th Century they had already taken to the air in the machines that Green didn't need. He wrote a novel 'The Brightest World' where a man flew on his own, just by the sheer will power. For this he was hounded by the government, as someone who had to be destroyed on the basis of suspicion only. How many times do we read such narratives? Why do we want to destroy those who dare to run on waves or fly on their own?

Waters near Salem are rather gloomy, and so are Hawthorne's books. But there are good people there. The legend of Frezi Grant, the young girl walking on waves, the one from Green's novel 'Running On Waves' also starts in a gloomy port where the ship 'Running On Waves' was embarked. That port very well could be Salem, from which it sailed along the shore to an even gloomier Dagon, an industrial city resembling Boston. After that it arrived to a place called Gel-Gew just in time for an annual carnival, which very well could be Rio or some Caribbean island. But I see it differently. I see the last stop as Salem, right in front of the Hawthorne's House. I see the statue of Frezi Grant, a beautiful girl with her hands stretched towards the sea. And I see it erected right on the Witch Hill or Gallows Hill as a glorious memorial to virtue, love. and hope. In the novel one of the Gel-Gew citizens says about the statue,
     "This town needed a vantage point. Now it has one."
     I felt the brotherhood in that town. It was good to be in the place that gave birth to Martha Corey and John Procter, those heroic souls who inspired Hawthorne, Green and Charles Upham. How similar they are, those good people, so far apart. So, I wrote a poem of the brotherhood I felt. After that I bought those super-tasty fruit candies in the store right in front of the House of the Seven Gables.

Image By
Alexander Korkin
ID:371057744

Chapter 18

Farewell

To him in whom love dwells, the whole world is but one family...

Buddha

Прощанье с Россией

Я стою у окна и гляжу на ирландский парад,
Где зеленые ветки покрыли поток демонстрантов.
Рыжеватые девочки ножкой о ножку стучат,
И католик поет Danny Boy, обнявшись с протестантом...

Этот маленький остров, как много людей он вместил,
Сколько выгнало их многолетней волной на чужбину..
Но они не оторваны-память скалистых могил
До сих пор помогает ирландцу в лихую годину.

Моя Родина, та, что огромной лежала землей,
Неизбежна, как смерть, что Набоков нам всем напророчил,
Почему же прощание стало моею судьбой?
И не будет для нас ни парадов ни песен уж точно.

Почему эмигрантам России и в мире утех
Не дано прикоснуться друг к другу в сообщности новой?
Разделение гасит едва пробудившийся смех,
И объятий не жди на дорожках, покрытых половой.

Почему же в России, такой необъятно большой
Не нашлось ни лесов ни полей, даже скал на границах,
Что связали бы нас, рассеянных по тверди земной.
Чья печать бы легла посвсеместно на изгнанных лицах?

Я прощаюсь с Россией один, не делюсь я ни с кем,
Этим мигом, что начался там, у порога родного.
С той землею, что общей была, расстаюсь насовсем.
Непрерывно, с утра до заката, все снова и снова.

Сколько было и будет таких же как я бобылей,
Свой покинувших дом от безумной крови государства..
Нет возврата назад для растерянных блудных детей
До отхода в последнее, светлое, вечное царство.

Видно только вот там, от всей жизни земной отойдя,
Мы узнаем друг-друга в тумане, на береге милом.
Задохнемся от слез, не стесняясь рыдать, как дитя.
Как же вышло, что нас лишь на это и только хватило?

Это будет потом, а пока я смотрю на парад,
По-весеннему ярко сияет ирландская зелень,
А напротив-стена, вся в потеках цементных заплат.
И березка под ней пробивается-прямо Есенин…

Farewell to Russia

I'm standing at the window questioning.
A wave of Irish green has caught my eye.
It comes around as regular as spring.
St. Patrick's Day parade is passing by.

"You're either Irish or you wish you were,"
They boast in all their revelry and joy
Both Catholics and Protestants concur.
As raffishly they sing "Oh Danny Boy."

A tiny island, homeland for the clan,
Though sadly forced by famine to depart,
They knew the cliffs of home would, to a man,
Remain so vividly within the heart.

It's strange, but from my homeland which is vast
Fled immigrants like me as from a curse.
Our only wish? We might live down the past
Parades for us would only make it worse.

Why Russian natives never coalesce,
With Russia's claim of camaraderie,
Aware division leads to loneliness,
Is something that I simply cannot see..

While Russia's vastness doesn't call us back,
Or here in exile help us to unite,
We're left with but a future that is black,
Alone and angry, coping with our plight.

On stepping from my Russian porch, I knew
In bidding my farewell, I'd be alone
I was aware my options would be few,
And my farewell, I'd endlessly intone.

From blood and madness, flight was our concern.
We were but loners from insanity,
Just children lost with no hope of return
At least until we face Eternity.

Perhaps, it's only then that we'll be free
To recognize each other as a friend,
Like little children in their infancy,
To live in innocence that knows no end.

But that is for the future, now it's cold,
And I must face a concrete wall of strife.
But wait .the slightest crack and I behold
A tiny Russian birch tree showing life.

Russian-immigrant community in the US is vast but by far-the most fragmented. None of the 'waves' communicates with another. Moreover, there are no ties between different immigrants who emigrated in different time periods. In the first verse, of the 'Welcome to the Family' I tried to make a connection to all the Russians here but in vain. They are too different. There are Russians and there are Jews. The 'old' Russian immigrants are primarily religious Christians, Russian-Orthodox or at least they claim to be.

Jews are the former Soviet Jews. They are the majority and the first thing they do is to pretend to be more American and more Jewish than locals. That means that they desperately try not to understand the locals, but to copy them and copy them at their worst, not at their best. For years I studied Russian-speaking publications and haven't ever noticed a slightest tendency to connect to other immigrant communities, to share visions and experiences or to exchange useful knowledge. Xenophobia prevails in those publications and those of us who know English well enough are between the rock and the hard place. That is we are alone. It is much easier for us to join Irish festivities than to participate in the celebrations of our own kind. I like Irish parades and whenever possible I join those at least as a spectator. There seems to be an astral connection between Russia and Ireland. Russian name Patrickey, definitely comes from St. Patrick.

The Irish parade goes on in its green glory, Catholics and Protestants alike. They sing 'O, Danny Boy' and greet each other as brothers in destiny. That is, of course, due to Eire. Not only is there a mystical connection between the shore cliffs there and the Irish souls, but it is as if the Mother Eire is always present. Every Irishman lives his life in a form of a River dance. No matter whether they are the first, second or third-generation, they are connected like a chain and those green branches over their heads make for the Irish forest.

Russia is much bigger than Eire. Long ago, when I was a child, we had a song in which the text was, "Our country is so vast. We have an abundance of forests, seas and rivers. This is the place where a man breathes free." Free or not, it so happened that when we left it, there was neither any way back nor any connection to keep. All that land stopped being ours. Even those who go there frequently on business or for pleasure do not really consider it theirs; they are just opportunists.

In 1996, when I came to Moscow for business I decided to test myself. I exited my hotel and just went down the street alone. That street I knew very well. In 1980 I lived there. So I decided to stroll down the street the way I had strolled hundreds of times before.. And I couldn't. I couldn't force myself even to buy ice cream. I was afraid that my Russian would disclose that I was a foreigner. I was afraid that I had an accent. I was just simply afraid, to be among my own people. They were not my people anymore.

All those rivers and forests, those seas and cliffs, they had not developed an eternal connection for all of us. How did that happen? The poem doesn't answer the question. It considers the fact. I also think that most likely, for the Russians the moment of truth is not in this life. Whoever said, "To be a Russian is a destiny"—was probably right.

Image By
Berkomaster
ID:555005572

Chapter 19

The Nonreturner

To see a world in a grain of sand and heaven in a wild flower.
Hold infinity in the palms of your hand and eternity in an hour.

William Blake

НЕВОЗВРАЩЕНЕЦ

Какое прекрасное русское слово,
Ни на каком языке его нет,
Осмысленно, строго и очень толково
Поставлен вопрос и получен ответ.

Куда-то поехал, зачем-то рванулся,
Под тридцать, под сорок или пятьдесят.
И ни через месяц, ни год не вернулся,
Как будто пропала дорога назад.

А раньше как было: морские походы,
Земельные споры, а то и война,
За дымку веков уходили народы
И не возвращались во все времена.

Не то современность-железной петлею,
Сковали границы земной горизонт.
Лишь тайные тропки остались изгою,
Ночные побежки на беженский фронт.

Удел отщепенцев, удел одиночек,
Цыганская доля отдельной души
И все полицейские службы хлопочут,
Чтоб больше ей некуда было спешить.

Наш дьявольский век уничтожил свободу,
Ту главную силу, что движет прогресс.
Поставил плотину на чистую воду
С бумажными ружъями наперевес.

И все же, когда наступает погода
И сходят лавины в далеких горах
Друг-друга приветствуем мы на дорогах,
Где нету возврата ушедшим во мрак.

Мы ведаем истину: наши стремленья
И есть основное, что нам лишь дано.
Мы-совесть и честь своего поколенья,
Живое броженье, святое вино.

Что нового в мире? Закрыли границу?
Поставили мины на горный туннель?
Но не задержать перелетную птицу,
И змейка проникнет во всякую щель.

Улыбка пророка, свободное слово,
Любые запоры откроет всегда,.
Мы приняли путь наш за первооснову
И не возвратимся уже никогда.

The Nonreturner

A word in Russian for the lost road back
A word that speaks of flight with no return.
Consoling thought for those gone off the track.
With no concern for bridges they might burn

At forty, fifty, matter not the age
On impulse, with no designated goal
Not as in fright or even in a rage
With naught but thoughts of freeing up the soul

I wonder how it might have been before
Explorers built their ships and went to sea,
Creating in their wakes the scourge of war,
From which the innocent are forced to flee.

The former free made it known,
Now manacled by borders in our way,
That for the single hiker on his own
Escape would be by night and not by day.

The rogue, the gypsy and the malcontent
The independent souls that sought release
From all the protocol hey underwent,
Content themselves confusing the police.

Our devil's century destroyed, I fear
The driving force of progress we began,
With dams when water should be flowing clear.
With paper rifles to disrupt our plan.

We meet upon the roads, with weather fine
As free as avalanches in their flight
And knowing we could never toe a line
We regroup in it
The wisdom and perceptions we possess
Are something lesser humans never see.
We are the honor and the consciousness
Of everything a human ought to be.

And so, with borders closed and tunnels mined
The bird of passage freely takes the air.
The snake will find his way, though much maligned
And in the end, the two become a pair.

The prophet smiles for yes, he knows no clocks
Return would come with much to great a cost
With obligations to the laws and locks
He makes his way along the road that's lost.

There is an unexplained phenomenon of Russian nonreturners. In all other countries people who emigrate for whatever reason-usually return to visit or just to show the old country to the kids, but not the Russians. Yes, sometimes people go back; I went back two times. But statistics say they come for a short time and practically never return. Originally, the 'nonreturners' were the people who left Russia illegally and couldn't return. Legend calls Prince Kurbsky, the Russian nobleman of the times of Ivan, The Terrible to be the first registered nonreturner. He escaped to Lithuania from the Tzar's wrath. Peter the Great's son Aleksey was a nonreturner for a long time and lived in Venice until Peter launched the 'Big Hunt' operation luring him back to Russia where he was tried and executed. Nicholas Turgenev, the prominent 'Decembrist', a member of the anti-Tsarist plot in 1825 remained in England and didn't return to Russia where he was tried in absentia and sentenced to death. He had to stay in England for the rest of his life. Alexander Herzen, the very prominent Russian political journalist had to leave Russia for good and published in England the 'Bell', an opposition magazine. He never returned. The last mass return of those considered nonreturners to Russia in the beginning of the 20th Century resulted in the revolution. So, that's why after it the victors made returning nearly impossible. Several hundred of the most prominent Russian educated people were forcefully deported. Most of them never returned even for a visit.

Eventually the nonreturners started to seek each other and exchange the experiences. As it turned out, it was not just a Russian phenomenon; Albert Einstein shares the honor. I read once in a Russian book that when the WWII was over, a group of German physicists sent a representative to him, asking him to come back to Germany and lead the new German physics. Einstein listened politely and then said only one thing:

"Give my best regards to Max Laue."

Laue was an esteemed scientist. Whether the story is true or not, Einstein never came back. Were there any nonreturners in the US? Charlie Chaplin comes to mind, also Gore Vidal, though both came back for short visits.

Nonreturners constituted a lot of people; the expats, the ones who live in countries different than their own. Moreover, even in your own country you can become a nonreturner if you turn on your free spirit and join the club. This is the club of the best people in the world; the ones who never stop being free.

Image By
Katja Gerasimova
ID:528137485

Chapter 20

The Reciprocity

Long ago, when I was studying English, a name was mentioned in our literary studies—Edgar Allan Poe. Strangely, in Russia he was mostly valued as a prose master, a writer, not a poet. Maybe it was that way because his verses were translated before the Revolution in 1917 by all those pre-revolutionary 'decadent' Russians thus casting a shadow on the original author. In any case, the first Poe's story I read was Murder on the Morg Street. The protagonist detective was the predecessor of Sherlock Holmes. Only later I read the beautiful translation of The Raven by C. Balmont and many other verses. In this country I reread Poe again, this time trying to translate one of the verses myself in order to understand the poet better.

Alone
Edgar Allan Poe

From childhood's hour I have not been
As others were, I have not seen
As others saw-I could not bring
My passions from a common spring
From the same source I have not taken
My sorrow-I could not awaken
My heart to joy at the same tone
And all I loved-I loved alone.
Then-in my childhood-in the dawn
Of a most stormy life-was drawn
From every depth of good and ill
The mystery which binds me still-
From the torrent, or the fountain-
From the red cliff off the mountain-
From the sun that round me rolled
In its autumn tint of gold.
From the lightning in the sky
As it passed me flying by-
From the thunder and the storm-
And the cloud that took me the form
(When the rest of heaven was blue)
Of a demon in my view.

Одиночество

Я с ранних лет был не такой,
Как все, я вечно был чужой
Не видел ничего кругом,
Что видели другие, в чем
Мои ровесники, друзья,
Искали счастья, ну а я
Не пил из общего ручья,
Но в темной глубине болот
Искал источник чистых вод,
Родник чудесных чувств и снов,
Что душу пробудить готов.
Так на рассвете жизни я
Испил из чаши бытия.
Природы вечной тайной был
Приворожен и весь свой пыл
Направил на чудесный мир
Из туч и звезд, речных стремнин,
Из молний, Солнца и Луны,
Что так обманчиво видны:
Сегодня есть, а завтра нет,
Закат идет сменить рассвет
И в небе, ясном как пророк
Витает Демон-одинок.

When I translated this I was amazed by how all poets were alike. They all are alone, unique, special. Michael Lermontov was alone through all his short life, so were Gulliame Apollinaire and Oscar Wilde. The last time I saw Joseph Brodsky on TV, he was alone in his place, burning old papers in the fireplace. Why is that they are so unhappy, so miserable, so lonely? I tried to find out more about that. I probed many sources and the only meaningful explanation I found was a statement by obscure Russian poet Nikolai Glazkov, "Poet is the slave of his freedom." He can't help himself. Young Edgar Allan Poe looked at the beautiful sky and the clouds that formed a figure of a Demon only for him. Most likely, he was familiar with the Demonian of Socrates, that eternal source of wisdom and creativity, which took its toll in the form of concentrated emotions and eternal strife for freedom. Moreover, the poet is free by definition; he can't release himself from an obligation to propagate this freedom to others. Alexander Pushkin said," I praised freedom in my cruel times." So did Edgar Poe. So did Robert Frost. So does Wendell Berry. There are hundreds, maybe thousands of those people who remain alone in the crowd.

Chapter 21

The Last Challenge

The greatest challenge to any thinker is stating a problem in a way that will allow the solution.

Bertrand Russell

Последний Вызов

Мне кажется, я будто снарядился
В поход альпийский, горные ботинки
И ледоруб, и крепкую вееревку-все
подготовил, уложил, проверил,
Присел перед дорогой-и забыл, зачем готовился.
Я что-то должен сделать-это точно. Мне говорят-
На горную вершину хотел подняться. Быть того не
может-в одиночку
На гору не взбираются, по-новой надо
Мне все пересмотреть.
Вот книга в вещмешке, в углу–вторая. Их надо прочитать..

Нет не наверх, а вниз я путь наметил, необходимо
Спуститься в кратер-здесь недалеко, но должен
я это сделать
Сам посмотреть на этот ад, что ждет меня так долго.
Мой последний, мой главный вызов, вот теперь пора..
Я не боюсь.

The Last Challenge

It seems I am prepared to climb the Alps.
Ice-pick and rope all checked and packed but yet,
Though ready to ascend their snowy scalps,
What is it I've prepared for? I forget.

It's something I must do, there is no doubt.
If it's ascend, should it be tried alone?
A check of goals to see what I'm about.
Perhaps two of my books will make it known.

It's not up there. It must be down below.
Decent, alas, is what is called for here.
The crater waits, and really, I must go.
It's time to face the challenge without fear.

While writing this book each co-author faced his own challenges

I, Mark Labinov (a.k.a Mark Sashine) am also a scientist, an engineer, PhD, PE and Certified Energy Manager. I specialized in thermodynamics and before the emigration I worked on a specific phenomenon I discovered. Then in 1989 I had to put all that aside and work as an engineer to establish a family. For some time it seemed I would never return to the work I loved. My father, also a scientist, reminded me of my discovery from time to time. The revival of that effort coincided with the death of my father and the starting of this book. I had to repeat everything from scratch and I also swore not to abandon this book no matter what. The challenge to balance two projects, each being a life commitment seemed insurmountable until I adopted the attitude that the book was a part of my preparation. I had two heaps of the books on my desk all the time; the ones on literature and the ones on geothermal power because it occurred to me that my scientific discovery could lead to a practical application. I had to read a lot of material about rocks, minerals and volcanoes. That coincided with the studies of style and poetry, all of which was new to me. It was very complex and tore me apart, but at the same time it did seem that I was ascending or at least preparing to do so. The book was progressing, and I became less and less afraid of that magma down below.

Now the book is complete. The preparation is over. Those volcanic rocks are very far from being friendly still, but I had achieved one of my goals without compromising another. It molded me and I have no fear. The book made me fearless. It is time to descend into the inferno.

FREE VS LITERAL TRANSLATION
By Hal O'Leary

For the past several months, I have undertaken the dubious challenge of attempting to translate poetry written by the Russian poet Mark Sashine from Russian into English. I refer to the challenge as dubious because I can't help but wonder if any interpretation resulting from translation can be counted on to represent the true intention of the poet. Some of the more famous yet questionable translations have admittedly strayed from what might have been the original intent of the poet. I cite the attempts by the many translators of Omar Khayyam's quatrains all with considerable differences in interpretation. The differences seem to suggest that some of the translators differed even in what they arbitrarily decided must have been Khayyam's basic philosophy, there-by making it obvious that they had inserted elements of their own thinking into the work. Edward FitzGerald undoubtedly, the most famous of these translators with his The Rubaiyat of Omar Khayyam, gives us this insight in a quote from a letter written to the noted translator of Persian poetry, to E. B. Cowell,: "I suppose very few People have ever taken such Pains in Translation as I have: though certainly not to be literal. But at all Cost, a Thing must live: with a transfusion of one's own worse Life if one can't retain the Original's better. Better a live Sparrow than a stuffed Eagle." I'm sure that there is a transfusion of my own life into any translation of Mark's poetry. I do believe, however, that our basic philosophies, Mark's and mine, seem to be remarkably alike.

The foremost difficulty in translating, I have found, is in dealing with idiomatic expressions, sayings, and colloquialisms. These, along with certain metaphors make literal translations absolutely impossible. I've also heard the terms "free or loose translation" unfortunately described as being not completely accurate or not well thought out, suggesting a restatement done casually. I take issue with that thought. I believe that a free or loose translation is mandated if one is to approach anything like accuracy in terms of the poet's intent. A well thought out translation often calls for deviation from or substitution for a specific or unfamiliar idiom. In either instance the restatement is not done casually but with a most considered effort to be true to the author's intent.

Recognizing that a misunderstanding from mistranslated work can be worse than no understanding, it has behooved me in this challenge to seek out, to every extent possible, Mark's honest intent. I fear that anything else, intentional or unintentional, can amount to deceit.

A Lesson in Life

A lesson that I learned long ago
Is something that I think you ought to know.
No matter what this life may have to show,
Should it be something you think is below
A standard over which you'd like to crow,
A standard you would rather not forgo
Here's something that will set your heart aglow.
When peers demand a stifling quid pro quo,
It's something that you needn't undergo
With just one little word you can bestow
Upon yourself a gift to help you grow
Into the man you'd be so proud to know,
The secret is to emulate Thoreau.
Just stand your ground and tell the bastards NO.

THE END

About the Authors

Mark Labinov, a.k.a Mark Sashine is a Russian émigré-engineer, PhD, PE, CEM. He writes fiction in English since Y2000 and his stories were published in Literary Hatchet, Thoughtnotebook and others. He is 61 years old and lives with his wife Maria in Asheville, NC.

Hal O'Leary, the Honorary Doctor of the Humane Letters of the West Liberty University, distinguished poet, theater director and scholar, the WWII veteran, has numerous works published including the Y2016 'Poems of Wit and Wisdom'. He lives with his wife Julianna in Wheeling, WV.